Forew

This is a book that would not have been possible without the love and guidance given to me seventy years ago by my grandfather Arthur Earl. The wealth of knowledge he shared with me in regard to caring for and sharing your life with dogs has made it easy for me to live my life in the company of the most amazing dogs. My grandfather was a shepherd who trained dogs for other shepherds. I have never known a stronger or more gentle man. He used that gentle nature to allow the dogs he was training, to learn everything they needed to know. I never ever saw him become annoyed or heard him raise his voice to any human or animal. He was a perfect example of how decent people should conduct themselves. I am sure that without his input I would have been a lesser man.

So am I an expert when it comes to training dogs? No. Do I think I know enough to tell other people how it is done? No! Now in my seventies am I still learning? Yes. All I will say is that I have found that treating my dogs as my equal, working to learn with them has proved to be most rewarding. There is no I in we and together my dogs and I have surprised ourselves with what we have achieved together. If there is love, trust and mutual respect between two equal partners anything is possible.

This book is dedicated to

My Grandfather, Arthur Earl. He was a fine gentleman and taught me many things. I loved him always and miss him still.

My wife Margaret who helps me to live my life in the way my grandfather taught me.

The following poem expresses what Margaret and I would like to say to the dogs we have lost. I wanted to share it with you, the reader. Despite extensive research to try and find the author, I have to list the author as unknown. Whoever you may be thank you.

A very big thank you to a very kind lady, Sheena Ford from Nibblers, Patterdales FC for introducing us to the poem. Our prayers are with you and all the other people whose dogs have gone before us.

A Human's Prayer to a Dog

Thank you for your bark

Thank you for welcoming me home with a smile and a wagging tail

Thank you for your kisses and paws always given without me having to ask

Thank you for your silly antics when you shared your playtime

Thank you for lying next to me

Thank you for greeting me with a cold wet nose

Thank you for adopting me

Thank you for your patience when you waited for me to understand what you needed

Thank you for accepting me

Thank you for letting me be a part of your life.

Our love forever, your human.

Contents

Dad & Dave with Rex

CHAPTER ONE

Rex

As I progress through my seventies it occurs to me that my life has been influenced in many ways by the dogs who have shared my life. They all had their own personalities but, they all share one trait, loyalty. That is so unlike many of the humans who have crossed my path in the same period of time. Although there are special people who make up for the slights offered by the others.

Right from my very early days, I have shared great times with all the dogs that have shared my life. This story has to begin with a wonderful Alsatian called Rex. He was a big, strong, black and sable dog, he could have been a show dog, maybe even won Crufts, I was told his sire won the American version of the championships but, I am not aware what or where they were held.

Rex was perfect except that one of his ears had broken at birth, because of that it never stood up. Nevertheless, Rex was a real champion to me.

From the time I learned to walk holding on to him, Rex and I were inseparable. He was never away from my side at any time, waking or sleeping, right up until I started school. Even then I couldn't wait to get home to spend time in his company. I threw balls and he chased them, we had great fun. He was my only friend, I truly believed I didn't need anyone else.

This was because there was nobody who I felt was worth my time except for Kenneth Cairns who had been my playmate before we started school. Kenneth and I drifted apart when he had more choice in people to befriend. To be fair to the other children when they looked at me there were many reasons to bully this four-eyed, big-eared solitary boy. From birth I had been brought up by my grandparents, so as children do they picked on the only boy in the class who didn't have parents, I was often called a bastard, not true, but as life has taught me the truth is not required when people want to put others down.

I was constantly in trouble for fighting, I had my spectacles taken off my face and snapped in half, my large ears boxed and my broad Cumbrian accent mocked. I was a solitary and lonely child, but I didn't care because going home to my loving grandparents and my wonderful dog Rex was all I ever needed. I really felt surprisingly, you may think, that with my big dog by my side I was living the best life. In life, I have made some good friends who it is a pleasure to know but in my early years, I found that dogs and horses were by far the best companions.

So as I say preferring my own company and that of my dog Rex I would go my own way. Rex and I would wander the lanes, paddling in streams around the village, playing ball and Rex like most dogs I have known loved to chase sticks. As I got older we Rex and I would climb the foot-hills of the fells above the Eden Valley together. I never wanted anything more than the companionship Rex gave me. We just loved the life we were living and we never knew that it would end. Because when you are young you are not aware that things change.

This seems to be a good time to tell you that Rex was a very obedient dog, something I took for granted. However one day I had reason to be grateful for his unquestioning compliance with my instructions. I was returning home from school and for some reason, Rex was upstairs. He looked out of a bedroom window and saw me coming. He stepped out of the open window onto the sloping roof of the bay window below. To all intents and purposes, he was going to jump down and run to greet me. I was horrified as I envisaged him breaking all his legs as he landed. Mindful of my grandfather's instructions to me that you should give one-word instructions to your dog whenever possible I just shouted, "Back!" Thankfully, although I could hear Rex's claws, slipping and sliding on the sloping roof he turned round and obeyed me somehow making it back in through the window. When he got inside he had run down the stairs and we exchanged hugs and kisses. I was feeling great relief but I don't think Rex had any idea of the drama I had created in my mind.

Returning to my thoughts on how quickly things can change I was about to discover it will often be the case that things change for the worse. Sadly I came to see that as life has a way of kicking you in the teeth. I was about to find out the hard way that changes were coming. The changes were very quick and very dramatic. At the time I thought they were the end of any happy life that I might ever enjoy. For some time

I had been able to see that Rex was struggling on his back legs, he struggled to get up and sometimes he could hardly walk. The problem came to a head one morning, he simply couldn't stand up. His back legs were paralysed, all the adults knew he would never walk again. Naturally being young and naive; I thought something could be done. I wanted to stay at home with my dog but I was sent to school and the vet was called. I never saw Rex again. As I got older I understood that what the adults had done, was the last kind thing that could be done for him. Alsation's or German Shepherd Dogs, as they are now more commonly known often have a genetic fault from birth, which will result in paralysis. He couldn't be left to lie in pain unable to help himself. That was not the view I took then because quite naturally I wasn't mature enough to understand these things.

All I knew was that Rex was a good, faithful and loyal friend and I had lost him. Looking back I am glad that Rex shared his life with me. We had shared wonderful times Rex and I. The things we did together are still as clear in my mind as they were in those marvellous, days when he and I ran and played together, more than sixty-five years ago. I can't bear to think how awful my life would have been without Rex in it. However, when I came home from school and found out what had happened, I felt that my dog had been murdered. In my mind, the adults had let Rex and me down. The way I felt I could not allow them to do this to me again therefore I resolved that I would never have another dog. A childish response, but my only excuse is that I was a child.

CHAPTER TWO

Meg

After Rex had gone, time seemed to pass very slowly for me as I tried to come to terms with what I perceived as my loss. I was too young and selfish to realise that there were other people who loved Rex. It seems to happen that way when you are young. You have no real conception of time, so although I felt an age had passed since Rex had died, really it had only been weeks. So when my grandfather, a shepherd who trained dogs for other shepherds, came home with the most beautiful little pup, I was not surprised. The reason I wasn't surprised was that there was always pups coming and going from our home.

This was though a beautiful pup her name was Meg and although I didn't want to give my feelings away, I really liked her.

Dave with Meg

My Grandad said he wanted my help to look after her. Well, I thought that's alright because I don't want another dog, but I don't mind helping to look after one. So perhaps a little ungraciously I agreed to help. From then on it was my responsibility to make sure that Meg was fed and watered every day. I carried out these duties little knowing that my grandfather was giving me lessons in responsibility that would last me a lifetime.

After I had been feeding and watering her for a while my grandad suggested that I take Meg for walks. I agreed again, my thoughts were, I won't become attached to this pup because she is not staying. We were in the early 1950s then and money wasn't wasted on fripperies, like leads. So Meg's lead was a length of sisal string, no collar just the string. It was something that I had seen with other dogs so I thought nothing of it. The only thing grandad said to me when the first time Meg and I went out together was, "Don't let her pull you". So off we went, there were no incidents and after a few days, Meg was walking beautifully. Always to heel, and no pulling It soon became clear that she was clearly a very intelligent pup.

The time was passing by and as we went along grandad would suggest little tasks that I should carry out. Such as, "See if you can get her to sit, then try dropping the string and see if she obeys your instruction to stay," It was all like a game, it was great fun and this clever little dog learnt very quickly. At first, when I told her to stay, she would follow me. Grandad said this was good because some dogs had been known to run off when asked to stay. This Meg never did right from the start she was glued to my side. Suddenly without me realising she had become my dog. This was a very, very special time because we were forming a bond. We were together all the time, off on our own. Once again I was roaming across the fells above the village with my dog. By now there was no need for a string around her neck. Meg was obedient and walked happily to heel, we belonged to each other. Like Rex before her, she loved to run after a ball or a stick and bring it back.

We had a bond and that felt good. I had a friend again. My grandad was a wise man and he had known all along that this would happen. He knew that I would love this pup and in giving her to me he taught me many lessons. He taught me I could and would care for more than one dog, in my lifetime. I would also learn without me realising it, how to train a dog or any other animal with kindness. Other lessons he was teaching me were patience, tolerance, thoughtfulness and kindness. These are life lessons which have made it possible for me to live a very happy life.

Once again I had a loyal friend and companion, this meant my time was filled with happy days. How lucky I was to be growing up in what many of us believe is God's own country, The Eden Valley. On any day that wasn't a school day, Meg and I would go out with a bottle of tap water, this was a drink for both of us if we didn't find a stream. Bottles had cork stoppers in those days, not screw tops. In my pocket, I would carry a bit of bread and jam, wrapped in newspaper. In my other pocket, I would have scraps for Meg. We would lunch up on the fells. We would often drink the water from the streams that flowed down from above. Nothing ever tasted better. Sadly Meg's life was only four years long, or short if you think of it. It seems that Meg had a heart defect, people did not attend the vet regularly then, these days we go once a month, regular health checks, preventative care and medicine as they say. In those days the dogs just lived and died naturally. So it was without warning that one morning Meg just didn't wake up. She lay there looking for all the world as though she was asleep. Once again a loyal and faithful friend was gone. This time I was older. I was still sad but I was learning that this was the way of life. Once again I see this rather scruffy and lovable border collie in my mind's eye even after all these years. Because of this, I am able to embrace the happy memories that come to my mind.

It is I think, worth mentioning at this point, the main thing I have learned about training dogs is that when you think you are training a dog, you are both learning. This is because there is a mutual feeling that comes between you and that dog. That feeling is two-fold, a feeling of trust and respect. Without those two things, I find that there can be no forward progress. There is no question of spirit being broken in pursuit of obedience when I train my dog. This is because in this relationship the dog and the trainer want to please each other.

If you choose to use rewards, to encourage your dog to act in the way you want them to, I find that it is better if you always reward your dog even if he or she hasn't got things right. The reason I say this is that he or she must not look at training as a miserable experience.

Any time spent together must be enjoyable. I have always found that love, patience and fun bring the best results. There are no bad dogs, just bad owners. This I believe is what my grandfather was teaching me all the time.

CHAPTER THREE

Max

Almost immediately I had another pup, again my Grandfather brought him home. We named him Max. He was a black Labrador cross-bred, I am not sure but I think that his other breed was Border Collie. Once again I was responsible for training him and he proved to be a quick learner eager to please. His keenness and readiness to do what was asked of him made him a real joy to be around.

The scenario was still just a boy and his dog wandering freely around the countryside, wanting nothing more than each other's company.

Max was a free spirit, always inclined to take off on his own adventure but, just as quick to return. Some people might have said he lacked common sense because he was always getting himself into difficulties. For example, If there was a hole in the ground Max would fall into it. If he ever saw a gap in a fence he would run towards intending to go through it, only to find that it was too small for him to get through. I lost count of the number of times I had to free him from somewhere he had trapped himself with the words, "Silly dog!" on my lips.

Max just could not see a blade of grass flutter in the breeze without seeing it as something to chase. A bird flying out of a tree or a hedge was fair game, even though there was no hope of catching it. Foolish squirrels, always the red variety in those days, who never realised how fast Max was coming upon them, would take startled flight. They always got away. Having said that, Max could have claimed a moral victory the day he tripped and fell over a molehill that was close to the bottom of a tree. As Max hit the ground, tumbling head over heels, the squirrel sat on the ground looking at him in amazement, before slowly climbing the tree trunk, occasionally, looking back down over his shoulder, at what he must have thought was a very strange, very silly creature. Rabbits would run for their burrows when the saw him coming towards them. Fortunately, he never tried to follow them inside. It seemed that he lost interest as soon as they disappeared from view underground.

Max would come back from every walk with some minor injury or other, He would have pulled a tuft of fur out, scratched his nose, sprained a leg, or cut a paw. His ability to come up with a new injury each time we were out was quite beyond belief. That said he always responded to my whistle, and he came to me when I called his name. He would stay on command, always staying completely still until I called him forward. He simply ran as though he had to do everything in a hurry. One day he was running blindly without a care in the world when he ran towards a fence and when he got to it, he stopped too late and knocked himself out.

On that occasion, he ran into the bottom strand of a three-strand barbed wire fence. He tried to turn as he met it but he bounced back and the force he met it with catapulted him back through the air. He sort of twisted in the air, hit the ground hard with his head, and lay still, As I caught up with him, he staggered to his feet looking very bewildered. After I had checked him over we walked on slowly. I thought that this incident might calm him down, but I was wrong because when a bird fluttered up from the ground and off he went again.

Max was always willing to run and that would be his undoing. The only road in or out of the village led down to the school, Max knew what time I finished school and made it his business to squeeze under the hedge in our orchard and come down to meet me. On that fateful day he chose to run across the road just as our local teenage tearaway hurtled through the village on his motorbike. This lad whose name escapes me after sixty years had been told by many of the village elders, that he would, "Kill some bugger" if he didn't slow down and take more care. Well, he didn't kill some "Bugger", not that I knew what one was in those days, he killed my dog! And he broke his own arm when he fell off in the crash.

It says much for how unpopular this lad was, that the villagers all showed concern for my dog's welfare and mine, as I was clearly distraught at the sight of Max lying unmoving in the road, none for the lad. As he lay moaning on the ground one elder villager, probably the same age that I am now, said to him, "Tha can fend for tha sen lad, you've been looking for that!" We never saw our local tearaway again, he simply disappeared.

We buried Max in the orchard and I swore never to have another dog. I think I blamed myself for what happened to him. Should I have stopped Max coming to meet me from school? Would an older person have walked him on a lead, or length of string until he had steadied down and stopped having so many accidents? I don't know, but I do know that he enjoyed every day of his short life, only eighteen months old when the motorcycle hit him. As with all the dogs I have shared my life with, I still think of him and still miss his companionship. If I did let you down Max I am still truly sorry.

CHAPTER FOUR

The Dog with no name

Before I come to the second Rex that would come into my life, I should just mention that I kept to my word until I was about nineteen years old, I didn't have a dog. Then one evening as I was walking home from a night out at about 1 am, a huge dog of dubious and unknown origin loomed up on me out of the dark. The dog was growling deep in his throat and I was very doubtful that I would get past him without being attacked. Clearly a male, he was limping and he had a broken rope around his neck.

Taking my courage in both hands and calling on the god who protects fools, I knelt down on one knee and encouraged him to come to me. I was speaking softly to him. I was working on the principle that if I could gain his trust he wouldn't bite me. Basically, I didn't want him to know that he had made me feel frightened. It must have worked because instead of him ripping my arm off as I was expecting, the dog let me stroke his forehead above and between his eyes, I have always found this action calms dogs

At this point, I could see the many scars on his head and face. He was big, very big and lean and rangy, he had matted fur on his body. I had no idea what breeds he had in him. He looked like what it would turn out that he was, he as the Americans say, was a junkyard dog. Everything about him was shouting at me, just leave him alone! Of course, I didn't listen, I got hold of his rope and took him home. We arrived without a problem at about 2 am. The problems were still to come, some of them due to the fact that I lived in what they called at that time a bed/sitting room. I opened a tin of Fray Bentos stewed steak for him and then I put the contents in a bowl with some dry bread and put it on the floor for him. Clearly ravenous he wolfed it down, I then filled another bowl with water for him and he drank it. After he had eaten and slaked his thirst the dog walked across the room, lay down next to my bed and went to sleep.

I can hear the questions now, why did you feed him in the bedroom? That was the first problem, the description of the accommodations, "Bed Sitting Room" told you what you were getting. So in my case for £1.10 shillings a week I had a home. In order to survive and have use of electricity and gas you needed a supply of sixpences for the gas and electric meters. All this was affordable on my £5.00 per week wages. Everything in the same room except the bathroom which was shared with the other residents of the house, a total of eight people. Due to the lack of a separate entrance, we all came in through the front door. This would lead to the second problem because over the three weeks the dog was with me, he attacked all of those other people for coming near me. Fortunately, with me holding him back he contented himself with barking and snarling at them. It could have been really bad if he had actually bitten someone.

The next problem was the landlady. After receiving multiple complaints from her terrified tenants she arrived to give me an ultimatum. Putting it simply she told me that if I didn't get rid of the dog, she would evict me. Looking back I have to admit that she was right it was an untenable situation. If he was just with me the dog was as gentle as lamb, if anyone else was around he acted like a raving lunatic. There had been one exception to this behaviour. I had bought him a collar and lead because this was one dog who wasn't going to be running free. We went out for walks and he walked without pulling me but I had to avoid people. We crossed over to the other side of the road if anyone approached.

This procedure had worked well until one day as we turned a corner we came face to face with a small boy and his dad. The boy, as boys will, said: "Can I stroke him?" Then without waiting for an answer he did just that! I was horrified expecting the worst but the dog just wagged his tail and walked on. I breathed a sigh of relief but, I knew that 'one Swallow does not make a summer'. So when the landlady said her piece I knew that whether I liked it or not, the dog would have to go.

I did what I should have done three weeks previously. I took him to the local police station and asked if they had a report of such a dog going missing from anywhere. They told me that they had but they did not tell me from where. After telling me that I was lucky the dog hadn't ripped my throat out they took him from me. He was snapping and snarling at the two officers, as they took him down to the kennel under the police station. I am not ashamed to say that I had tears in my eyes when they took him away. It was only then I realised that I had never given him a name. Perhaps I thought that I knew deep down that he would never be my dog.

That should have been the end of it but about six months later I saw him again. I was courting Margaret at this time and we were saving up to buy our first house. I wanted to speed the process up so I had taken an evening job to supplement my savings. I was working in part of an old factory and as I walked across the path between the factory and a scrap yard which was on my left, I heard a dog start to bark. I looked left just as the dog broke free of his tether and as the scrapyard was still open, he ran out of the gate. He hurtled towards me then reared up on his hind legs put his paws on my shoulders and proceeded to lick my face. The owner of the scrap yard ran up saying, "I wouldn't have believed it if I hadn't seen it myself". It seems the police had told him about me when he got the dog back, telling him that the dog was gentle as a lamb with me. He said that he had thought that they were just winding him up. He and I became friends from then on. We saw each other often and over time he told me he had taken the dog from another scrap dealer about eight years previously after the other guy had beaten the dog half to death. After that, until he got out and spent three weeks with me there had been no gentleness in the dog.

After that, I saw the dog every evening and shared my supper with him. The scrap dealer said I had ruined him as a guard dog, but the dog and I didn't really mind. This situation carried on for about eighteen months until one evening I came to work and there was no welcome from the dog. I went into the yard and my friend told me that the dog had just gone to sleep and didn't wake up. We buried him together at the back of the yard. I never knew how old he was and he never had a name. But I have no doubt that he was my dog, in some way he had lived his life looking for me. When he found me he gave himself to me the only way he could. He was a great dog and a good friend to me.

After that, I would not have another dog until I was in my twenties and married. Somehow time slipped away and other things were occupying our lives. It wasn't a conscious decision to not have a dog, any more than when Margaret and I did eventually take one on we really gave any thought to it. It was the right time and it just happened.

CHAPTER FIVE

Rex the Second

The next dog I had, or I should say we had, was a lovely gentle golden coloured dog. He really was a very gentle and lovable dog. He was naturally obedient, and a wonderful companion for my wife Margaret.

He would not be her first dog because as a child she had two lovely dogs. One was a large Collie cross called Gyp. He was black and brown with a lovely nature. He was just the right dog for a young child to grow up with. Gyp went everywhere with her. When Gyp sadly passed away Margaret shared her days with her aunt and

Uncles dog. He was a lovely dog called Mickey. Mickey was a black and white Cairn terrier cross Margaret believes. Again Mickey turned out to be a good childhood companion. I really did not show much imagination when I said we would call this dog Rex. The main thing was that there was no problem with us having a pup because like me Margaret loves dogs.

That said we hadn't been looking to have a dog at this time in our lives because we both went out to work. However, a neighbour of ours had a dog who had given birth to six pups and he was trying to get those pups homes. The other five pups were black and very sturdy, the image of their mother. Rex, as we called him, was what was known as the runt of the litter. He had fluffy golden fur and he was very small and delicate by comparison to the other more robust pups. He had fine bones and very dainty feet which did grow bigger. No one wanted him, so we decided to take him home. As I said I didn't show much imagination calling this dog Rex. Luckily the name did seem to suit him and he always came when he was called.

Rex needed a lot of care and attention to rear him, but we were rewarded with affection and loyalty in return. Also although he was a small dog never growing very big, he had a lovely flowing golden coat which felt soft and silky when you stroked him. He was very eager to please and he spent more time with Margaret than he did with me. I was playing sport as well as working and I spent a lot of time training for my sport, So it could be said that I abdicated responsibility for the training of Rex and to some extent I left Margaret and Rex to enjoy each other's company. Having said that Rex was always pleased to see me, making a big fuss of me whenever I came home, likewise I really enjoyed his company.

However, there were times when Rex would get over-excited. Sometimes things would go wrong because of it. One day when he jumped up with the joy of seeing Margaret, one of his front paws caught her face and one claw made a small but deep cut on her cheek beside her nose. As Margaret said at the time it was nothing, more of a shock than a hurt. She has a small almost invisible silver scar where Rex's claw caught her. A little reminder of a dog that loved us both very much.

Rex was a dog who loved to have fun. He would take great delight in chasing and retrieving a ball. Rex kept his ball beside him at all times. As soon as he saw us go near the door, he would pick up his ball and follow us to that door in the hope that he would be going out with us. Of course, if we were going to work, for instance, Rex would be disappointed but good-natured about it. When we did go out with him Rex would trot along to heel, waiting for us to take the ball he was carrying in his mouth and throw it for him. No lead was ever needed as he was always obedient. There could never have been a dog who knew so much without being taught.

That said Rex did have problems. An example of his problems would be that he was easily agitated and any slight noise would frighten him. If a car backfired he would drop onto his stomach and lie on the pavement quivering. Before he would get up and walk on we would have to stroke him and talk to him, in order to calm him down. Another example would be if another dog barked anywhere near him, he would shake like a leaf and cower down. Rex really did suffer from his nerves and there was nothing we could do about this, except try to calm and reassure him. What we didn't know was this nervousness would turn out to be a symptom of something more serious, although it would be some time before we knew just what that was.

For quite some time everything bowled along as it always had if anything Rex seemed more timid as the years went by. It has to be said that he was happy in our company and we in his, the problem was he did not cope well if left alone when we went to work. His level of distress was increasing. It seemed inexplicable to us that he would be so calm we were there and when we came in but at the point of us leaving his agitation was high. We have often thought since that if we hadn't decided to move house Rex might have been with us longer than he was. Because of these feelings in some ways for his sake, it was a move that will always be tinged with regret.

However we had decided to move and of course, Rex moved with us. Sadly that was when things became really bad for him. He just couldn't settle in the new house which was much smaller than the one he had lived in for eight years. It has to be said that Rex was really suffering. We tried to understand why this was and his upset was being discussed daily. Then Rex started to have fits. This was a very upsetting visible problem, he would shake with so much force and thrash around foaming at the mouth, we knew that we would have to take him to the vet. He was in great distress and it was heartbreaking to see him in the throws of these fits. We would take him to the vets. Surely we thought the vet will have a treatment for this condition.

So we took Rex to the vets, they knew him well because he was up to date with all his injections. In fact, as with all our dogs, he was popular with nurses and receptionists alike, they were always pleased to see him when he came for his check-ups. After we had told him about Rex's problems I think the vet knew from the start what the outcome would be. He carried out a very thorough examination and set about getting to the root of the problem. Over the next week, we had various tests done and it was with some trepidation that we took Rex back for his results. The visit started badly and got steadily worse and ended with Margaret and I going home without Rex. The vet told us that Rex was suffering from epilepsy, he went on to say that the fits would become more frequent and more debilitating, there was no hope of him ever getting better, only worse. Rex would only get worse. Twenty-five/thirty years ago, there was no treatment for a dog who was suffering from epilepsy. Putting it simply, it was a death sentence for our lovely dog!

The vet said we could take him home in a state of sedation and have medication with us to keep him that way. Or------- We chose the or, we just couldn't bear to see him suffer, nor could we allow him to stay with us under sedation, for the selfish reason that we wanted him to remain with us and be part of our lives. That was no life for Rex to have to endure. The vet asked me to come into the other room with him, while he administered the lethal injection. When we got there he said stroke your dog and talk to him, it will help him to be calm. I did as the vet asked. I told Rex what a great dog he was and how much we loved him. I had no idea of time, minutes, seconds, but suddenly I heard the vet repeating my name, I looked at him and he said, "You can let him go now". I looked at him then at Rex who just dropped limply from my arms, I fell back against the wall, if the wall hadn't been there I would have hit the floor. I staggered out of the room to where Margaret was waiting, we left, in complete despair.

On the drive home, I told Margaret I would never forgive myself, I had let Rex down, in my eyes, I had killed him. She tried to console me and apply logic to the situation but even now as I write with tears in my eyes I haven't forgiven myself, for letting Rex down.

So once again I decided, I would never have another dog. Of course as with so many things in my life I was wrong. There would be good days to come, there would be other wonderful dogs, to share our lives. And we would be blessed by their love and companionship. That said not for the first time I wondered why my dogs seemed to leave me so soon. However I now know that it is always too soon when a wonderful and special person or dog has moved into the next room, before you, it doesn't matter how much time you have shared with them, it is always too soon.

CHAPTER SIX

Lucky

It is worthy of mention at the outset of this chapter, that due to the length of this special dog's life, there are many special memories to record. Therefore this will be an inordinately long chapter. I hope the reader will enjoy the memories I am sharing in spite of its length. It would not be fair if I knowingly left anything about this remarkable dog out. Because Lucky never gave less than all of himself to Margaret and me.

This time the way our next wonderful dog came into our lives was incredible, I might even say it even seemed impossible. His life story was so special that a biography of his life has

been written and published, to all intents and purposes by himself. If you doubt that is possible, I will re-ask the question Lucky asked at the start of his book, 'Lucky A Dog's Tale', "A dog can have a life story can't he?" This time the story is being told from the point of view of Margaret and myself. This is because the previous book was written and narrated by Lucky.

At the time we came to meet Lucky, about twenty-seven years ago, Margaret was working in Manchester. I used to drive her to work before, carrying on to my own place of work. On the Monday morning in question, we were almost at Margaret's destination when a door on the car in front of us opened, while it was still moving and a black pup tumbled out of the door bouncing hard as he hit the road, then he was still moving with the momentum gained from leaving a moving vehicle. He bounced, rolled over and over, came to a stop and lay still.

I stopped the car and while I watched the car that threw him out disappeared into the distance, Margaret got out of the car and ran over to the pup. By this time he was struggling to his feet, looking a little groggy, but hopefully okay. Margaret picked him and brought him to the car. They got in and she kept him on her knee, talking to him and stroking him. We carried on to Margaret's place of work and she took him in with her. I carried on to work, still thinking about what we had seen. We had been so shocked that I hadn't seen the registration number on the car. I didn't even know what make the car was.

Margaret would tell me later in the day that all they had to feed him on at work was a tin of cat food. This turned out to be a mistake as, a short time later he lost control of his bowels, meaning that Margaret had to clean up the mess. Nevertheless, he came home with Margaret. When I got home I opened the back gate and this little black ball of fur, who had the biggest feet I have ever seen on any pup, ran tripping over those feet up our long tree-lined path, to greet me. When he got to me he threw his front legs on to my knee and looked up at me. His eyes seemed to say, I want you, I will make you want me.

Lucky would greet me in this way for many years to come, although as time went by his front legs would dangle over my shoulders and his head would be above mine. Of course, I am only five feet seven inches tall so you may not agree that he was a big dog. Then again I am broad for my height, I have a forty-four inch chest, Lucky's chest was bigger than mine and his front paws were bigger than my fists!! So you may think not the biggest dog in the world but, big enough. But I am getting ahead of myself because there would be one hiccup before he actually became our dog. We hadn't decided whether we were going to keep him or not. There were two reasons for this one reason for being slow to make a decision was that we were both out at work every day. This would mean that Lucky would be alone in the house, the question that had to be answered was, would that be fair to him? The other reason was that we had a cat, Whiskey. We had taken Whiskey in as stray when she was a kitten and we didn't want her to feel put out. We needn't have worried on that score, they loved each other.

Margaret had discovered when she had fed Lucky the cat food at work that he could not eat properly, so because of that, she had been feeding him his Pedigree Chum puppy food off a wooden spoon. It turned out when we took him to the vet that he was too young to have left his mother, therefore he had not developed to the point where he understood how to get food from a bowl. He was somewhere between four and five weeks old according to the vet so it would be a while before he started to mature. Of course, sixteen years later he was still playing Margaret up, expecting to be fed with a wooden spoon. He loved Margaret so much that he clearly thought that he was doing her a favour by eating like this.

During the first week, we asked a neighbour if she would go in at lunchtimes and check on Lucky, she was kind enough to agree. Now Margaret while in conversation with the neighbour, mentioned that we will still undecided whether we would keep this as yet unnamed pup or try to find him a good home. This was a mistake and we would have cause to regret that mistake. The reason for our regret was that the neighbour took matters into her own hands. We were discussing the matter in the car on the way to work on Friday morning knowing that we had to make a decision for the pups sake. He was so loveable and he had clearly taken to us so we agreed that we would keep him. We decided that when we met after work as usual to do the shopping we would also get the things that the pup would need. At lunchtime, I phoned the vet, registered the pup and made an appointment to start his injections as he clearly would not have had anything of that nature yet.

We came home and opened the door, expecting the usual enthusiastic welcome from the pup. It was not forthcoming the house was silent, clearly, the pup had gone. We couldn't believe it. I went and knocked on the neighbour's door when she answered, I asked her, "Where is the pup?"

She replied, "Oh it's gone I found it a home."

"Why did you do that?" I asked,

"Well, You said you didn't want it". she said.

"That was never said", I replied, "Anyway Margaret wants him so you had better get him back."

"Margaret needs to make up her mind." was the reply.

"She has," I replied, "So please bring the pup back."

She went off immediately and quickly returned with the pup. As I pointed out to her later, if I had said I wasn't sure I wanted to keep the television, she would not have taken the TV out of the house and given it away.

We got over the disagreement with our neighbour and we remained friends until Margaret and I moved away, some twelve years later. There was a few problems after we got the pup back. The house where the neighbour had taken the pup had three boys living there with their parents; they were aged between ten and fifteen and did not appreciate the pup being taken away from them. Their disappointment resulted in an unfortunate exchange with the fifteen-year-old every time we saw them he would always start shouting, "That man stole our dog!" This went on for a couple of months until the youth clearly got bored of shouting at us. The joke was that they had only actually had the pup in their house for about fifteen minutes so they could hardly have become really attached to the pup. It has to be said that, Lucky, the pup was almost beside himself with joy when he came home to us. It was clear that we had made the right decision.

Putting that unfortunate incident behind us, we had decided to call the pup, Lucky, Because as Margaret and I said, we were lucky to have him, and he was lucky to have us. We could not have known just how lucky we were. We would enjoy every day with Lucky for more years than we could have dreamed of or hoped for. He set his stall out immediately and there was a hierarchy in the house. In his mind it was as follows; Dad, Lucky, Mum and then Whiskey the cat. He proved this whenever work took me away from home. Lucky would lie beside Margaret on the bed with his head on my pillow. He would lie lengthways as a person does. He would never attempt to even get on the bed if I was home. When he came our lovely cat Whiskey mothered him and he treated her like a mother all her life. When she passed away Lucky cried, whining and looking for her for days. We worried that he was not going to get over the loss of such a loved member of our family. Eventually, he did, but he seemed to need more affection than ever before;

Although we have said that Lucky gave us much happiness and joy throughout the years, we did experience some frustration during the early months. We can remember that as a pup Lucky would demolish a three-piece suite. He literally ate his way through it Although to be fair to him he only chewed his way through an armchair and a three-seater settee. My recliner was unmarked for reasons best known to himself, he simply left it alone. We persevered with this situation and only replaced the furniture when after six months he had grown out of this phase, young dogs usually do. When the new sweet was delivered the delivery driver was aghast when he saw the amount of damage that had been done. "What on earth caused that?" He asked. Margaret shrugged her shoulders and pointed to a very innocent looking Lucky who had already taken up residence on the new settee. "You have got to be kidding, I would have killed him" came the reply. Margaret just smiled, because in our eyes Lucky could do no wrong.

There were other things that succumbed to Lucky's mighty jaws. For example, books were pulled from the bookcase to be chewed and torn. Strange though Lucky seemed to have a most discerning eye or as he was chewing the books or should I say pallet? He was very selective; he chewed his way through Margaret's Catherine Cookson collection. He seemed to target them. He never touched any of the authors I had on the shelf. Dumas, Dicken's, Verne, Lamour and Stephen King clearly were not to his taste. He also had a predilection for shoes, women's shoes in particular as our friends Peter and Lynda found out whenever he stayed with them. They loved Lucky as much as he loved them so they forgave him. The other item he had a fondness for were my socks. He would carefully remove them from the laundry basket, then not chew them instead he would give them a serious amount of sucking. Explain that if you can I never could. After about six months he stopped chewing things although all through his long life he could be tempted by one of Lynda's shoes if she didn't keep an eye on him. The other thing was he always pinched my socks and kept them by him when he slept, he didn't suck them any more, he just liked having them beside him.

When Lucky was six or seven months old I would discover that one of the really fun things in my life would be training Lucky. This was because he was quick and intelligent. The fun part was that because Lucky had an independent streak, he could do things and learn quickly but if he got distracted he would do his own thing. However, initially, I lacked faith in my own ability to train Lucky as so many years had passed since I had actually worked with a dog. So Margaret and I decided to look for a dog training facility that we could take Lucky to. We wanted the best for him so having found a training school not too far away from where we lived with a very grand sounding name we decided to go. Due to the subsequent upset, I choose not to name them as they may still be in existence and doing a good job for other people.

We arrived at the training centre and paid £15.00 an hour which was a considerable amount of money nearly thirty years ago. We took the view that you get what you pay for and as I say the grand-sounding name led us to believe that we were giving Lucky the very best chance to have an enjoyable life. As the joke goes "What a mistake to make." The whole hour was a complete disaster, a waste of money and a complete waste of Lucky's time. It would be the only time in his life that for what was only a short space of time, he found himself being physically and mentally abused, by a man who I referred to on the day as the most vicious clown in Christendom!

Once again I won't allow his name on these pages this time because he in my opinion and that of Margaret is not worthy of having his name in a book about love and loyalty. We made a boisterous entrance with Lucky dragging us around the training area rushing to meet all the other dogs. This resulted in complete pandemonium, owners and dogs stumbling, falling, shouting, barking, whining and complaining. This did not go down well with anybody. Indeed some of the dogs unable to get to Lucky decided to fight among themselves. At this point Lucky, having lost interest in all the shenanigans was sitting quietly beside me with what I swear was a look of amusement in his eyes. One of the ladies who was supposed to be in charge said we need our big uncontrollable dog expert, someone please go to the office and get him. "Oh yes!" cooed his assembled fan base.

When I saw this clown arriving I should have gone back to the car with Margaret and Lucky and gone home. I am sorry but he was everything I would try not to be. He had a bald or shaved head, I wasn't sure which. He had pallid complexion and what used to be termed a five o clock shadow. He had a huge stomach hanging over the waistband of his leather trousers, wearing a muscle T-shirt and he was wearing sixteen lace hole Doc Martin boots to complete the ensemble. He walked towards us, his fleshy tattooed arms held away from his sides as he strutted his six foot plus body towards us. I decided wrongly to give him the benefit of the doubt, not judge a book by its cover. Muscles was clearly looking to dominate the dog and his owner, "Give me his lead" he said, "I will soon have him under control."

He immediately dragged Lucky off his feet as Lucky got up he did it again looking to his admiring audience for approval. They obliged. "Look at that, they cried." "The dog is learning who is the boss." When this happened the second time Margaret started to cry, she couldn't believe that anyone would want to hurt any dog, let alone her dog in this way. Before she could speak we saw that at that moment, the boss was on his knees. There were gasps of disbelief from the admiring throng, because Lucky, unable to comprehend what was happening to him, had resisted. His resistance took Mr tough guy off his feet. As he fell he lost his grip on the lead and Lucky walked calmly back to me.

Muscles got to his feet and launched a foul-mouthed tirade of abuse at me and Lucky. He followed that up with the words, “That dog is out of control. I will need him to be kenneled here for at least two weeks.” going on to say, “The only thing dogs like him understands is a good beating.” I looked at him taking my time in replying, then I spoke. “ The only beating my dog will get is over my dead body” I paused, then continued, “I don’t think that the miserable excuse for a man that you are can do anything.” “In fact as you clearly are the biggest clown in Christendom I would just shut up before you make a bigger fool of yourself”. “I wouldn’t continue standing there in front of me full of bluster, because face it, you are not up to the job of putting me in the ground”. “So don’t make empty threats”. Muscles glared at me and then swore at me, with that he turned away from me and walked back to the office.

Margaret and I took Lucky back to the car and went home. As we drove Margaret said, "What do we do now?"

I replied, "I will apologise to Lucky and then he and I will train each other."

I have never subscribed to the view that brutality will work on any animal. In my opinion, the clowns who think that they can use their perceived superiority to beat them, or rub their noses in it mentality of training, are not fit to breathe the same air as any animal that has ever walked the earth.

I felt there was a good chance of success of being able to make a training programme work because Lucky was never disobedient. He just acted like a free spirit and if he was chasing squirrels or any moving thing, none of which he ever caught, he just couldn't hear you. You may remember that I lost a dog to an accident, a few years previously because he didn't pay full attention, I couldn't let that happen again. I had to find a way to get Lucky to concentrate. What I would not do was break his spirit. He was going to be my friend and my equal. I didn't know it then but Lucky would live a long life and never be subservient, to me or anyone else. He became the most gentle loving dog you could ever wish for. Lucky never let me down, he just shared our lives and made them better.

I decided that if Lucky was going to get the idea of paying attention we would have to go out early before I went to work. This would be before other people got up to take their dogs out. Lucky simply couldn't see another dog without racing to say hello and make friends. Not too bad you might think but when I tell you that where we walked him was quite hilly countryside with a farm and a riding school across from each other you might see the problem. For example, one day we were at the top of a hill and looking down we could see a man walking his dog two fields away, Lucky was off like a shot ignoring all my shouts and whistles to return. That was another thing, I don't like the sound of my own raised voice so things would have to change.

Lucky and I started going out at four am every day, most times Margaret would still be asleep and not wake until we returned. The first morning it was still dark and as soon as I let him off the lead and he ran off into the darkness. I knew he would not come back to me if I called his name so I just kept walking in the direction he had run. This took me down from the first field, under the disused railway bridge into the wood. As dawn came up I caught sight of him, running backwards and forwards through the trees. I could see he was worried, he couldn't find me. I kept walking, he was always in sight now and he wasn't getting further away because he kept doubling back on himself. Suddenly he became aware of me, I don't know if he saw me or picked up my scent on the breeze. Lucky's reaction was immediate; he flew to my side tail wagging and sat at my feet. Looking up at me. I told him he was a good boy and stroked his head. There was no point in shouting at him, I know I wouldn't have wanted to come back if I had been abused when I did return. We walked on and he never went more than two of his body lengths away from me. We both enjoyed a lovely walk.

We had made a good start, the days and weeks went by, I let Lucky range further away from me but, never out of sight, his response to my whistle became immediate. I needed more because Margaret can't whistle, so I resolved that Lucky and I would try something different. He had developed a habit when he trotted ahead of stooping and looking back over his shoulder to see where I was. I would use my arm to wave him on. So, I thought could this clever dog so eager to please understand that if he saw my raised arm he should return to my side. I had no doubt that if he chose to he could.

Lucky's response to this new idea was amazing, he understood what was required and would run back to me, whenever he saw my arm raised above my head. We were ready, by now to let Margaret see what we had been doing and let her share in the fun Lucky and I was having. That is the way with Margaret and me with our pets, they become part of the family, become mum and dad to them, when we speak to them. So I said to Lucky it is time to bring your mum out with us, let her see how clever you are. It was a Saturday morning 10am, four weeks after I had started this step into the unknown the three of us went for a walk. When we reached the fields, I let him off the lead, he ran around always returning and sitting at my feet when I whistled him. Margaret was delighted, she made a big fuss of him telling him he was a good boy every time he returned. Lucky was a really good boy. He never caused me a moment's pain in his entire life.

So off we went, I like to think Lucky was as excited as I was, we really had something to show her. When we had been out for about twenty minutes, I thought right, it is time to surprise Margaret. So I sent Lucky on ahead, he ran down the hill towards the railway bridge I encouraged him to keep going on ahead with my hand, every time he looked back. Margaret and I remained at the top of the hill, Margaret was worried that Lucky was getting too far ahead and said so. Don't worry I said just raise your arm, which she did. When Lucky, who was always paying attention, saw her he bounded, with great enthusiasm, back up the hill, and sat down beside Margaret. This excellent result would be the start of many years of happy walks for us all.

Margaret would, because she finished work earlier than me, now be able to take Lucky out every afternoon for the next sixteen years. Something that had not looked possible when Lucky and I started to train each other had actually happened. Lucky was six or seven months old at the time and the clever dog that he was, he had helped to shape his own destiny. I wonder what Muscles would have thought if he could have seen this dog so eager to please, responding to kindness, not brutality. Actually thinking about it I don't think he would have been interested, it would have required him to see reason and I think he was long past having the ability to reason. I content myself with knowing he never got near our lovely dog again. I do wonder looking back if I should have called the RSPCA so that other dogs were protected from him. I regret that my only thought was to get Lucky away from him. Hindsight is a marvellous gift that can bring out a guilty conscience in most reasonable people.

Of course, there would be problems because there always are when you have dogs but these problems were not of Lucky's making. One really big problem was a Dalmatian who just couldn't help attacking every dog he saw. He cost his owners a lot of money in vets bills that had to be paid on behalf of the other dog owners to put right the injuries their pets had suffered. From the first time he saw Lucky when he was out walking on the lead with me when Lucky was about eight weeks old, he would run at us snapping and snarling. Fortunately, Lucky became very good at evading this dog and never had an injury inflicted on him. From my point of view, I was really pleased that Lucky's temperament was such that he would take evasive action before he would fight. He was growing bigger and bigger but at the same time, he was growing gentler and gentler.

As Lucky got older we found that there was another dog, a huge Rottweiler, that attacked Lucky every time he saw him. This dog's owner was a muscular bald-headed man, he thought it was alright for his dog to attack Lucky or anyone else for that matter. In fact, he actually thought it was funny! It was always me who had to get hold of his dog's collar and drag him away from Lucky. The guy would laugh and say that Lucky and I were soft and frightened, I just bit my tongue although I did once tell him he was a clown who needed to grow up and control his dog. That just prompted a stream of abuse as he walked away. This went on until Lucky was about eighteen months old. I didn't want to find another place to walk, Lucky liked it crossing the fields, playing in the brook and running through the trees. After all, we lived there. To this day I have no idea where the guy and his Rottweiler lived. So this unfortunate situation continued, until one day we met on the path through the woods. As we were going in and the Rottweiler and his master coming out, it seemed that we were heading for the usual scenario, or so I thought, but Lucky had other ideas. As always the Rottweiler ran and lunged at Lucky. But Lucky did the strangest thing, instead of trying to run as he usually did, Lucky moved quickly forward crouched low, and went under the dog grasping one of his hind legs in his jaws, then he twisted, throwing the Rottweiler on his back. At that point, Lucky just put one paw on the dog's chest looking down at him. No biting no snarling, nothing, Game over.

When I called him off, Lucky came and sat beside me. The Rottweiler lay for a few minutes clearly shocked. The owner was shocked, it was clear that all his normal bluster and bravado was gone. He was just looking at Lucky and I, he seemed to be seeing us in a new light. The Rottweiler got up and he and his owner slunk past us, we never saw them again. They must have gone for a walk elsewhere. After that there was only one other incident in sixteen years, another large dog, a Weimaraner, ran at Lucky with what was clearly malicious intent. Lucky just stopped as the dog approached and looked at it. Whatever the other dog's intention had been he just lay down. He must have thought better of it. Lucky was never again attacked by another dog. He was a big lovable gentle dog. He thought everyone was his friend in his whole life. Lucky never bit or hurt anyone or anything, putting it in the only way I can he was a real gentle giant.

Of course, pet owners have responsibilities and we have always tried to take those responsibilities seriously. With that in mind, Margaret thought that having Lucky neutered was the sensible thing to do, for health reasons. I am sure other dog owners are aware that there are various cancers that are possible for dogs. That is if they remain as the expression is entire. Plus the fact she did not want him running around after the local female dogs, in those days and now there are far too many unwanted dogs. We didn't want to be responsible for contributing to that situation. However our vet was not keen to do the operation so soon because, as it was clear that Lucky was going to be a very big dog and he, the vet, wanted to wait till Lucky was two years old. His reason for this decision was to avoid the chance of deformity while he was still growing. I didn't altogether understand this but we decided to listen to the vet and waited. It was during this visit to the vet that we found that Lucky had webbed feet. So we now knew that he was a Labrador/ Newfoundland Cross, hence his size. The way he was built it was clear that he would have been a large example of either breed. As it was he was very big indeed.

So the big day came and Lucky went in for his operation. He was as I say a very big dog by now and this meant that he had to be heavily sedated. Margaret and I were very worried, it turned out to be a very long day. After wondering and worrying all day we were both relieved when the vet phoned to tell us that we could bring him home. When we got to the vet's surgery we found that Lucky was very groggy and unsteady on his legs. We were told he would be alright but that we had to keep him warm and monitor his condition through the night. The reason for this was because he had required more sedation than they had thought he would. It seems that he had fought with all his great strength to remain awake. The vet said it didn't matter how late it got, if Lucky's temperature dropped we must phone him, on his mobile. Well, it did and I phoned the vet and told him that Lucky was ice cold. He said, "I can't do anything at this time, I am sorry but you will have to do whatever it takes to get him warm.

The central heating was on, but that was having no effect. He remained freezing cold. We covered him with a blanket with no change to his low temperature. Lucky's breathing was laboured and I knew that if I didn't do something quickly he would die. In the end, I had a brainwave, I knew what I would have to do. It was the only thing I could do. I lay down and got under the blanket with him. That would hopefully mean that the heat created by my body would be transferred to Lucky. I lay down beside Lucky all night, at some point, I fell asleep. When I woke in the morning this great and incredibly powerful dog got himself up. I was delighted to see him on his feet. I was even more delighted when he drank some water and then looked for his breakfast. When he had eaten his breakfast he wandered out into the garden. For myself, I felt really ill but I was glad to see Lucky looking so well. He completed his recovery and thrived.

The vet phoned me to check on Lucky that morning and was very pleased with the news. After that seemed as though Lucky and I had built an unbreakable bond during that night. He became even more devoted to me than he had been before.

Now as big as Lucky was growing he was a very agile dog. One day he gave us a demonstration of a remarkable feet of agility. The birds used to fly across our garden from tree to tree and sometimes en-route would land on the bird table, they normally flew at a height that was usually just above my head. Now I'm about five feet seven inches, that is quite high for what happened. On the day in question, Margaret and I were standing in the garden talking to our neighbour Geoff, over the fence. Lucky was lying quietly at my feet. Suddenly without warning, he took off vertically.

Now, remember he was my height if he stood on his hind legs. Well somehow from a lying position he rose above that height and caught a bird in flight. When he landed and let it drop from his mouth, it was unharmed although it was clearly shocked. The bird took a few minutes to recover himself then flew into a bush. Geoff just looked at me saying, "I don't believe that" "Neither do I replied". Margaret was standing there shaking her head in disbelief. It was not just that Lucky had done the impossible in catching the bird, the really amazing thing was that when he caught it in his great powerful jaws he didn't hurt it. Another example of how gentle Lucky really was.

Really that shouldn't have surprised me because I already knew that Lucky had a gentle mouth. He had developed a habit of rolling my forearm/wrist in his mouth when I reached down to stroke him when he was lying beside my armchair. It seemed to be a way that he showed affection. Although I could feel that his jaws were powerful enough to crack the bones in my arm, he trusted me to know him well enough to trust him and know that he wouldn't do that to me. There was another time when people who were visiting doubted that he had a really soft mouth. So because I believed in him, without knowing what would happen I put an egg in his mouth and told him to carry it to Margaret. Lucky did this and Margaret took it off him, there was not even a crack in the shell. In case you are wondering no it hadn't been boiled. It was a fresh egg, which to prove the point I cracked into a glass and drank it raw, I like raw eggs in milk so that was no hardship.

There was one thing I would have preferred that Lucky did not have in his mouth horse apples. He thought it was great fun to pick one up and bring it to me, at first I wouldn't know what it was he was bringing to me and I would let him drop it in my hand. For those who don't know the term horse apples, it is a polite name for horse manure, you may have seen that horse droppings are in a ball or apple-shaped pieces. Be that as it may, I didn't want them in Lucky's mouth or in my hands. Lucky grew out of it I think the scent attracted him for a while in his younger days. He always looked so proud when he brought me my gift. I would find out in a few years that there are worse things a dog can do with for want of a better word, manure.

Of course, he did once demonstrate how powerful his jaws were. I had been buying from the pet shop the pig's ears they sold for dogs to chew on. Lucky demolished them very quickly so

I asked the guy at the pet shop if he had anything that would last longer. He said that he had some pigs Trotters. So I bought two. I don't know how he cooked and treated them but he said one of them would last Lucky a week. It amounted to the foreleg of a pig from the knee down. I took them home and gave Lucky one, he took it and closed his jaws on it, whereupon it shattered to a myriad of razor-sharp pieces. Which I quickly picked so that he didn't swallow any of them. So it was easy to imagine what he could have to my forearm if he chose to.

Not long after that demonstration, we took Lucky on holiday to the Lake District for the first time. Margaret had found a cottage to rent in the village of Bothell, near Kendal. When we arrived at the cottage Lucky treated it like his home from home. He really loved it there, completely relaxed and happy to be there. Most days we would take him to Bassenthwaite Lake when he would run down through the trees and plunge in. He loved the water he would jump in and swim the width of the lake and back again. Lucky was a very powerful swimmer. The first time he went in and set off across the lake Margaret said to me, "What if he gets in difficulties?" I was competing in triathlons in those days so I said,

"I will swim out and help him." That was never necessary; he was the strongest swimmer you will ever see. After all his forebears were water rescue dogs. For Lucky, swimming really was just a way to have fun. We used to go up there twice a year because as a Cumbrian born and bred, I just loved being on home ground. After that first trip, Lucky would get the scent of Bassenthwaite Lake through the open car window and we would have to stop before we ever got to the cottage, just so that he could have a swim.

Then our days would follow a similar pattern, breakfast, then in the car with towels to dry him with, and the usual bowl for Lucky's bottled water and off to the lake. After that it was off to Allonby Bay at Silloth, to walk on the beach there. Of course, at all times home and away there would be play. Lucky loved to play hide and seek, chase, find and catch balls. One of his favourite pastimes was a tug of war. Using a special toy bought for him in the pet shop. Even holding my end with both hands I was hard-pressed not to be pulled from my feet, Lucky really was an immensely powerful dog. Even allowing for his size he still had a disproportionate amount of strength. Lucky was gentle and compliant by choice, he could never have been forced into submission hie strength wasn't just what you saw on the outside his mental capacity made him stronger.

When we made those visits to Allonby Bay we discovered a very strange thing about Lucky, he really didn't like loud noises and he, when the waves were crashing in would start barking, he simply would not go into the sea. Especially if the tide was coming in. Strange for a big dog who was such a strong swimmer. I think he thought the sea was shouting at him. So we timed our visits to coincide with the tide going out. Lucky loved running along the beach. Incidentally, he didn't like the sound of fireworks or thunder either.

We had some great times and had been going to our cottage and having trips out from there to Allonby Bay for a couple of years. Then an unexpected disaster very nearly worked out very badly for Lucky. This is what happened. We had developed the habit of pulling off the road at a car park next to a chapel. Then we would walk over the sand dunes and down to the shore. There was a boggy area, it was just along from the chapel which for some reason, really smelled strongly of petrol, I never did find out why. The day would come though when I would find out just how deep it was.

Margaret, Lucky and I were coming back from our walk along the beach. The tide had just started to come in. That meant for the reason I have mentioned, it was time to go home. Just as we set off back to the car, Lucky put up a rabbit in the sand dunes. Now Lucky had never caught a rabbit and that didn't change on this occasion. But at his fastest pace, flat out he shot out of the sand dunes and straight into the stinking swamp.

It all happened so quickly before I could even whistle Lucky he was in the bog. Immediately he sank up to his neck, his size and weight on this occasion worked against him. Fortunately, he showed great intelligence and stayed still. He didn't struggle at all. Without thinking I ran into the bog, I was sinking with every step, I knew I had to try and keep moving or I would get stuck myself. Now I knew how broad Lucky's chest was, the depth, breadth and girth of it. So I knew that I would only have one chance of lifting him out. I plunged my arms into the sludge and when I straightened up and lifted, by some miracle when I straightened up he was in my arms. I turned my body and threw myself towards the firm ground on the bank. Seeing that Lucky was on firm ground I let him go and he slipped and staggered towards Margaret. I was half on the firm ground and managed to drag myself the rest of the way out.

Both Lucky and I stank to high heaven, we were completely covered in the foul-smelling slime. I couldn't drive in that condition so there was nothing else for it, we would both have get into the sea and wash the scum off. We walked back over the sand dunes and into the sea. I swam out in my clothes, then started to swim parallel to shore, it wouldn't do to drown after all that. The water was freezing cold, it is after all the Solway Firth. When Lucky saw me plunge into the water he followed me, this was the only time that he ever swam in the sea. We came out cleaner, but even with the taste of salt and the smell of it, there was still the smell of petrol coming from both of us, it must have penetrated our skin. Clearly it was in our pores. We went back to the car now because I could not drive or even sit in the car with my sodden clothes, I would have to change. First things first, I vigorously towelled Lucky dry. Even that action warmed me up a bit. Then I poured him a bowl of water. Now it was my turn to use one of the many towels we always carried in the car. We never knew when Lucky would fancy a swim so we had to be prepared.

While I was doing that Margaret was rooting around in the car, looking for something I could wear. Success: she found a pair of shorts and a T-shirt, also a pair of trainers and an anorak. I would be fine, with the heater on in the car. Unfortunately, there was still the smell of petrol on Lucky and I. We did not get rid of that smell until we got back to the cottage and had a shower, the first time I ever showered with a dog but it was the only practical thing to do. We all walked along that beach many times over the coming years, I am glad to say that Lucky never went anywhere near that swamp again. Once again Lucky and I had strengthened our bond of friendship by an experience that came our way.

Taking a trip down memory lane several years after that event, Margaret and I returned to Allonby Bay in 2016. We walked along the beach and when we came over sand dunes on our way back to the car, we looked for and found the foul-smelling boggy area, it has never changed, it is still a foul-smelling area in an otherwise beautiful place. Why it is like that or even why it has never been filled in or sorted out, we don't know. One thing is sure, we had some great days with Lucky on that beach, over a number of years. Even that foul-smelling bog is part of the happy memories we have of Allonby Bay.

Dave with Lucky

Another place we used to go with Lucky when we were up in Cumbria was The Trout Hotel in Cockermouth. This is a grand spot, Bing Crosby used to stay there when he came to Cockermouth for the fishing. The Hotel is on the River Derwent and Lucky would swim in the river before we relaxed and had lunch at one of the outside tables on the bank of the river. Many happy days were spent there just relaxing in the sun. Every one our days in Cumbria were worked around Lucky and we enjoyed them all. He swam in the River Eden at Lazonby and we walked the fells east of there, in and around the village where I grew up, Renwick. We even went back to live there for a while. In those days we would sometimes have a drive over to Hexham Racecourse to watch the horses run. These were great days with Lucky in his prime.

Sadly, life would take him away from us in the worst way that I could imagine, it started with me having to go into hospital with Sepsis. Margaret said that Lucky spent all his time lying on the floor watching the door, expecting me to come through it. He would jump up in anticipation when anyone came to call. Hoping to see me come in. When I didn't arrive home, after a while he just stopped getting up.

When I recovered Margaret told me that after I had been gone for a few weeks it had got to the point that Lucky wouldn't even raise his head. He wasn't eating, he wouldn't drink his water. Lucky was fading fast and Margaret had no choice she had to call the vet. When the vet arrived he examined Lucky then he gave Margaret his diagnosis.

"This dog has given up, I don't know why but what I can tell you is he will never get up again putting it as plainly as I can he is slowly dying. The only kind thing I can do for him is to put him to sleep."

Margaret was devastated, she could not let me know she had to make the decision there and then. Margaret knew I would not want Lucky to suffer so she decided to let him go. She got down the floor and hugged Lucky and told the vet to do it. While the vet prepared and then gave Lucky the injection she continued to hug him and told him how much we both loved him. Lucky slipped away knowing that he could not have been more loved,

When Margaret told me, I responded as she knew I would. I told her she had made the right decision, but that I was sorry she had to make it alone. I was in shock and during the next five years when we didn't have a dog, I never really accepted that Lucky was gone. It seemed that I couldn't mourn him because I hadn't seen him go. I could see his casket with his ashes in, on my, tallboy in the bedroom, with the lovely ornament of a dog that looked just like him holding his lead in his mouth every morning. I also knew that when we are gone Margaret and I have decided to have our ashes and Lucky's scattered together on the shores of Bassenthwaite Lake. None of this ever made his passing real for me. For it to become a reality I would have to wait another six years, making a total of eleven years in denial of reality.

From Lucky's point of view, the only loss he had ever suffered was our cat Whiskey and he had felt that loss deeply. In his mind, I will always think that he viewed my absence as being the same as Whiskey's something which I wouldn't be coming back from. I think he gave up his life with the idea that it would bring him back to me. He was special and there is not a day goes by that Margaret and I don't speak of him and he is still loved and missed.

In concluding this chapter I can only say, how pleased and proud Margaret and I are that this wonderful dog shared his life with us. Lucky enhanced every day that he spent with us and loved us as much as we loved him.

CHAPTER SEVEN

Bruno

It was very hard to contemplate having another dog after Lucky and for several years almost six in fact we held out against the idea. One day Margaret asked "do you think we will ever have another dog? "Probably" I replied. Well, she said, "We are getting on in years, I don't think we should have a pup". I agreed. We decided to look on The Dogs Trust website and found a few we liked the look of at the Darlington rescue centre, and one we thought would definitely not suit as it was a huge dog in a dreadful state.

We drove to Darlington one Saturday morning and spent the day being disappointed. Margaret had asked, "How will we choose?" "We will take the dog that chooses us" I replied. None had and we approached the final cage, without much hope, there was a Husky whose name I don't remember who did not appeal to us and we did not appeal to him. Then Margaret said, "There should another dog, a German Shepherd cross in here as well, his name is Bruno, I will call him." She did and out of the back sleeping area came a huge gaunt dog with his tail wagging, it was the dog we had discounted on the website. We looked at him and without hesitation, we both agreed that we should take him for a walk around.

We went back to the office and arranged to have him brought to us, we have never made a better decision. That first walk was a joy in spite of his size. Bruno did not pull me when we got around the paddock to what they call the summer house and when we got there we went in. We had been told we could let him off the lead in there, we did and sat down. Bruno rolled on his back indicating that he wanted his tummy rubbed, I obliged and Margaret and I agreed that he would be coming home with us. This was, without doubt, one of the greatest decisions we have ever made.

We took him back up to the centre and the kennel maid took him back to the kennel while we did the paperwork. We also had to listen to all the reasons why Bruno wasn't the dog for us. He will pull you over when you walk him on the lead. This was because I had been knocked down by a forklift truck sometime before, and I was not very steady on my feet indeed, never would be. Strange then that I have walked him up and down the paddock and he hasn't pulled me. Then it was, well you will never be able to let him off the lead because he ran wild in County Kerry for two years and no one knows where he was before that. I held my counsel on that. Eventually, it was decided we would have him, the adoption talk done, the £100 paid willingly and the paperwork done. Bruno was ours!

Then they said you can come and take him home a week today. "Oh no," said Margaret, "We are not leaving him here that long". We would have taken him there and then but Bruno had to have a medical and an injection before it would be possible for him to come home. We would have to be patient, so it was agreed that we could pick him up and take him home on the third day. Filled with happy anticipation we arrived back on Tuesday eager to see our dog. We parked up then we went into the centre. After a short period of time, Bruno was brought to us by a kennel lad, who said, "I will take him to the car for you because he probably will fight against being put in the car". I went ahead and opened the back door of our RAV 4. Bruno saw me and the open car and took off in a great leap landing in the back almost dragging the lad in with him. The lad's response was, "I think he really wants to go home with you". That was probably the understatement of the year. We drove home with a very happy dog in the car. The only downside of the journey was that a pheasant ran into the radiator of the car on the way home when we were going along the dual carriageway. As I write this some years later, I have cause to remember that pheasant and the fact that it was the Tuesday after Easter Monday.

We arrived home and as we entered the house, one thing or should I say two things that had given us pause for thought when considering having another dog appeared. Our two cats, Brandy and Oscar arrived to welcome us home. They saw Bruno and ran from room to room with him in hot pursuit. Up the curtains and on top of cupboards went the two cats. Once up there they held the high ground and Bruno lost interest. In a few short days the three became the best of pals, comrades in arms. Indeed in the woods at the back of our home the three became the best mousers and Bruno's case the most unlikely mouser. There were several occasions when the cats would chase the mouse into Bruno' mouth.

He would then come into the house and open his mouth letting the mouse go. He was so gentle, he had huge jaws but the mice were always alive. Then Margaret and I would have to catch them and let them go. The mice would be in shock and so would be easier for me to catch them and put them back outside.

The next thing was to help Bruno to learn to run and walk free, then return to me. We enjoyed many happy hours in the woods and the top meadow as he was always eager to please. He proved that he would never leave my side. There would be ups and downs while he disciplined his own mind, as to what was within his capabilities. An example of this came quite early on in the process. Bruno slipped while he was running through the woods in the rain and hurt his right hip. He got up and limped to me leaning heavily against me, expecting that I would be able to help. I did my best and we limped home. It was just after Easter so getting a vets appointment was a nightmare and the visit to the vets was worse. In future years, the time following Easter in relation to Bruno was destined to be heartbreaking, but I will stick to this incident for now.

Dave & Margaret with Bruno in 2016

I got the appointment at a vet not too far away from where we lived and took Bruno in to have his hip checked. It is an appointment that I was sorry I made Bruno attend if I had my time over I would have taken care of him myself. The appointment went wrong from the moment we arrived. "Oh," said the person at the desk, "He is very big". "Yes," I replied proudly, "Almost 5ft at the shoulder, 6 ft 7 ins", on his hind legs but as gentle as a lamb". "Well the vet who is in today is frightened of big dogs." was the response. I won't dwell on the horrendous experience that followed but it involved a muzzle, a huge person knocking Bruno on his side and kneeling on top of him, while he was examined.

The poor dog was bewildered, so I spoke up for him, "Just get off him and let me take that muzzle off him, We are leaving!" "Well just give him some paracetamol for the pain, I don't think his hip is broken". Said the vet, "Pay on your way out". I was furious saying, "Well if his hip and his ribs are not broken it is no thanks to your heavy associate dropping their knees on him." That experience cost more than £60, they never got their hands on my gentle giant again. In his whole life, Bruno never attacked, bit or hurt any living creature. I am so sorry I let a pair of charlatans muzzle and hurt him.

I was telling the lady who works at the pet food stall at the market in Kendal, what had happened and she advised me to take Bruno to the Westmorland Vets, "They are wonderful with big rescue dogs." She said. How right she was, We saw vet Mary first, she was gentle and kind. Then she introduced him to the lady who would be his nurse, Jane, she saw Bruno every month for the rest of his life. Again gentleness and kindness were her watchwords. He was weighed on each occasion as we had taken his weight up from 32 kilos, he was very underweight when we got him. We like Jane very much but Bruno grew to love her and always went in through the vet's door eager to see her.

No criticism of The Dogs Trust they were caring very well for him, he had been in an awful state when they got him. We had gone too far because he weighed 62 kilos. He looked great but that weight was not good for his heart or his back leg joints. We got his weight down to a constant 46 kilos and he thrived. The care he received was exemplary from all the staff, Vet's Paul and Gerard tried their very best to ensure that he lived a long, healthy and happy life. Also, there was a lovely lady there called Sarah who used to kneel down and give him cuddles, whenever we went there.

Every day spent in Bruno's company was a joy. Friends adored him and he adored them in return. He always welcomed everyone who came to our home with a bark like rolling thunder, then he would lie down happily when they came in. Our friends Joan and Pat doted on him. He enjoyed many happy days in their company. It was the same with my sister Christine and husband Dennis. They would visit with their collie, Molly and we all enjoyed great days in their company.

Once I had Bruno's trust our walks through the woods were a joy. He would run free chasing rabbits and squirrels, never catching one but loving the chase. Early one morning out the mist came a huge stag, it saw us and ran, with Bruno in pursuit. It leapt a fallen tree, Bruno couldn't do that and so the chase was over. The run was over in seconds but what a memory, what an incredible thing to see. We went on our way, Bruno's need for exercise helped me to walk better than I could have dreamed, always in pain but the pleasure gained in his company was worth all that. Bruno would always trot ahead but then he would stop and wait for me before moving on once more. Not bad for an untrainable dog who we had been told would always run away if he got free. No one had allowed for the fact that he was blessed with inherent loyalty to those he loved and who loved him in return.

There were days when Margaret, knowing that we followed a circular route on our walks would come out to meet us from the other direction. When she came with hearing range she would call Bruno to her. He would look at me and I would say, "Go on find your mum". He didn't need a second invitation, he would leave me to race to her side. They would make a fuss of each other and then he would run back to me, the old slowcoach. He was a wonderful dog, loving, loyal and true, he never let me down, at any time or in any place.

I sent the Dogs Trust at Darlington a photo of Bruno practising the stay position in the woods, I think they were impressed that he had become such a loyal friend and much-loved member of our family. That a dog who had run wild for two years with no traceable history could become so faithful and reliable. I will always think that he had looked for Margaret and me all his life, he like we, became complete when he found us. He might not have known who we were, but when he found us he knew we were the right people for him. We certainly knew that he was the right dog for us.

We had a real scare in 2018 when we found a long hard lump on Bruno's side. We took him to see our vet, Paul, who told us it was a tumour, it would have to be removed. Paul did the operation successfully removing the tumour and Bruno thrived. When he recovered if it were possible he was stronger and quicker than he had been before. It seemed that our fears and worries that we might lose him were unfounded. He was always happy in our company as we were in his. Our friends and neighbours, Martyn and Jayne, have two dogs Bob and Ted, small terrier types, they loved going for walks with Bruno and with them. These were happy fun-filled days that we thought would never end.

On one occasion we had a visit from our niece and her partner Phil, they brought their dog, Ivy, is a small Patterdale terrier to visit us. Once again Bruno displayed his gentle side. He was kindness itself to Ivy, allowing her first place at the water bowl and his place in front of the fire, he really was a gentle giant. Always trustworthy, always reliable, always gentle. He was an amazing dog, he made every day special because of the pleasure he took in the life he lived,

When I started to write this book in early 2020 I was sure that Bruno would be the last dog to share our lives. After all, we were in our seventies, Bruno was a very young and active dog in our view, just approaching ten years of age. Our experience with our previous dog, Lucky who lived to be sixteen years old, led us to hope that there were more wonderful years to come in Bruno's company. Indeed when he had his medical check-up in February, the vet, Paul commented that Margaret and I were doing all the right things and that he thought there was no reason that Bruno wouldn't be able to live for at least another five years. We were boosted by the fact that he felt the same confidence as us. We could not in our worst nightmare have anticipated the misery that only a few more weeks would bring.

In the week approaching Good Friday, Bruno was as strong and as fit, as he had ever been, he was enjoying his walks and chasing and retrieving his toys. Squirrels, rabbits and birds who landed close to him were in peril of being chased. Of course, as usual, he never caught anything. I truly believe that he loved the chase with no intention to succeed in catching anything. There was nothing in his behaviour that could have given us the slightest inkling of the horror that was to come.

On Easter Saturday inexplicably he slowed down, he still wanted his walk but he didn't run or chase. He suffered no loss of appetite, and his toilet function appeared normal. When he rested instead of choosing his normal places on the settee or at the end of the bed he would lie at our feet with his head using my foot as a pillow. Sometimes he would stand looking at us with such love for us clearly shining in his eyes as if he was trying to tell us something. As I said he still ate, he still went for his walks but squirrels, rabbits and pheasants did not have to flee from him. He would find no pleasure in the chase, He carried his toy but did not want it thrown for him. We were worried and the vets were closed because of Covid-19 or he would have already been to see them, Easter or not.

Easter Sunday dawned and our friends Gareth and Kat called on us with their son Ethan. They had not met Bruno before but as always, although they stayed outside the gate for social distancing purposes, Bruno was welcoming and patient with the boy who just wanted to make a fuss of him. He would welcome the lad's attention then return to my side, returning to Ethan occasionally when he called him for brief moments of attention. But he was always making his return to me. They left and Bruno had his tea time meal, followed by at his insistence his walk.

Before I went to bed I looked at Bruno and saw that his stomach was swollen, I felt it noting that it was hard. I went to Margaret who was already in bed saying, "I am calling the vet in the morning no matter what and explaining why". She agreed and got up and went to see him herself. As she said he looked so frail it made her feel afraid for him. The following morning I phoned the emergency number we had been issued with and discussed the situation with Gerard. He took account of all I told him and as Bruno was still eating and performing his bodily functions he said he would see him the next day. I took the earliest possible appointment at 9pm the following morning. In the meantime, Bruno continued eating and going for his walks and his bodily functions were working fine. We hoped that whatever it was would not be serious.

When I got up at 7am as usual the following morning Bruno was eager for his walk, although he did not run around at all. Once again his bodily functions were fine. We came back from his walk and Bruno was disappointed to find no breakfast waiting for him. I explained to him that it was just so he could have his check-up, there would be breakfast for him when he came home. Margaret knew we were leaving but just watched from the window as he jumped into the back of the Rav 4. Off we went for what I thought was his outward journey. In my mind, there was no conceivable reason that could prevent Bruno from coming home.

We arrived at the vets and parked in the car park. The arrangement was that I should phone on our arrival and someone would come out to us. I did this and when there was a reply we were told to wait until Paul was free. While we waited for Paul to come out I sat on the tailgate of the car and Bruno lay his head in my lap. I stroked him and told him what a wonderful dog he was. Even though the vets were taking emergencies only, there were four cars ahead of me in the car park all with pets and their owners waiting to see the vet before me. Bruno and I waited patiently and as soon as it was possible Paul came out and called for Bruno Lodge. This is a lovely way that the vets practice, recognise that the pets they treat are part of people's family. I stood up and Bruno jumped from the back of the car, then stood beside me while Paul examined him. He agreed that Bruno's stomach was very swollen. But was unable to really tell me anything without a scan. So with that Paul said, "I will phone and tell you when Bruno has had the scan." Then he walked back into the surgery. Bruno trotted beside him and for the first in his life, he left me without a backward glance.

I drove home where Margaret and I waited for the phone call that would tell us what the problem was. We speculated, of course, thinking that even a treatable heart condition would be a good result. Eventually, after what seemed like an eternity, the call came. It was Gerard, the other vet, calling on Paul's behalf. He told us the news that there was a lot of fluid on the scan and they thought that they could see a tumour. He made suggestions about the next step, of course, we put ourselves and Bruno in his hands.

Margaret and I were in shock, we continued to discuss the situation with Gerard and took the decision that there would have to be an operation. Bruno would never be stronger than he was now because, for whatever reason Gerard said he was dying. Bruno was already under an anaesthetic, so the operation just had to be done. A couple of hours later Gerard phoned back he told us that Bruno was still in surgery and that there was no hope. Gerard had pumped seven and a half litres of blood out of Bruno's stomach. He had found that there was a tumour on an artery and the artery had burst. He had removed the tumour and repaired the artery but then they had found another tumour on his spleen. As he continued to look he could see that there were more tumours all through his stomach. Gerard had fought and tried as hard as he could but as he said, "There just isn't any hope". He then asked the question, "What shall I do?" Margaret and I took the decision to do the last kind thing we could for Bruno and let him slip away without him being revived from the anaesthetic. This great-hearted dog, a gentle, loving, giant with the heart of a lion and the strength of an ox had left us too soon.

That should all there is to tell you but the strangest most wonderful thing happened. Something that you may or may not believe but I don't mind if you can't accept it because I know it is true. A couple of days later Margaret was out in the garden and she turned around when she heard the gate open, there was no one there, she went and closed it, then came in and told me about it then went back out. A few minutes later I was just sitting in my chair looking at our two cats Brandy and Oscar, who were lying asleep in front of the fire. Suddenly I saw a translucent shape in front of me, I thought, "What's that?" It became clearer it was tan and black and the shape lifted its head, the eyes were the most solid thing about it. As it looked at me I realised that it was Bruno. He was standing there just looking at me as he often had before. I called out to Margaret "He's here!" Margaret came in asking, "Who's here?" and walked straight through him and he was gone. People are entitled to think what they will, but I know Bruno came home and I thank God for that because it showed us that he knew his rightful place to live had been with us. Bruno also must have known that I was in complete despair because I felt that I had let him down. I believe he wanted me to know that it was alright, the love that was always in his eyes was clearly there as he looked at me for the last time.

I find it very strange as I look back to think that we got Bruno at Easter and the pheasant died on the way home. The only time Bruno ever knew pain in our care was when he fell and hurt his hip once again at Easter. Then when he sadly died, it was Easter. As hard as I try I can't explain it. Margaret and I are just grateful that Bruno shared six wonderful years of his much too short ten-year life, with us. He was everything a good dog should be and more. I will just say that I feel I mourned him so deeply because suddenly I was mourning Lucky as well. It was as if the flood-gates of emotion trapped since Lucky died were finally released so that I could mourn two of the greatest Pals a man could have. As with Lucky, we have Bruno's ashes in a casket now and when Margaret and I shuffle off this mortal coil, the four of us will have our ashes scattered together.

Our two cats, Oscar and Brandy, mourned for Bruno as well and still looked out for him months later. For weeks Oscar was in complete despair, if there was an open door in the village Oscar would look in it for his lovely gentle big brother. We could not move Bruno's blanket because Oscar was sleeping on it. The scent of his protector, his safe place comforting him. Brandy was never off my knee; he was just not his usual independent self. Both cats were losing weight. We were worried for them. Little did we know that something in fact someone was coming that would save us all.

Bruno

CHAPTER EIGHT

Bentley

I decided in my infinite wisdom, that I would inform The Dogs Trust at Darlington where Bruno came from that our lovely gentle giant was gone. They were very sorry to hear the news and were most sympathetic. In the course of conversation, they told me that due to Covid-19 they were struggling for funds. I was sorry to hear that and would certainly make a donation. That I thought would be the end of the matter. How wrong I was. They asked if I would look on their website at the dogs that needed help. I agreed and that set in motion the following very rapid chain of events. Having looked at the dogs The Dogs Trust had available for us to sponsor Margaret and I chose a dog at Liverpool. He was a German Shepherd crossed with a Newfoundland, called Bentley. Again we thought that is it, job done. There was more to come in the near future. The next question we were asked was if we would come and see him when isolation was over and that seemed okay so we agreed that we would. Was that it? No. We were then asked if it would be alright if Bentley was brought to us by a van on Tuesday? They would take him back if we didn't like him or thought he might be too much for us. We could not allow this dog to be taken back. So a week to the day after Bruno died, Bentley arrived and what an arrival it was! The van pulled up and the side door opened then, a bundle fur and fun burst out of his cage and made himself known!

Bentley had arrived and I took him for a walk because I knew he would need a wee after the journey. Then of course he needed a drink of water. We did the paperwork with the young lady who brought him and then she left Bentley was ours! The fun started straight away. We have as mentioned two cats, Brandy and Oscar. Bentley could not wait to introduce himself to them. First of all, he leapt at Brandy in the hope of a chase. Brandy is the original cool cat, he will not run from anything or anybody so he reared up on his hind legs and bopped Bentley on his nose. Game over. Then Bentley saw Oscar coming up the path to the open front door, great he thought and ran at Oscar, who obliged by running around the garden, before jumping a five-foot high wall. Bentley followed suit, leaping over the wall with ease, now he was in the woods and it didn't look as though we would be able to catch him anytime soon.

Margaret was in dismay watching helplessly and shouting any name that came in her head – Lucky, Bruno, then David! – I came out and Margaret made me aware of the situation. I did the only thing I could and called Bentley more in hope than certainty. I was not disappointed, he leapt the wall back into the garden and stood in front of me wagging his tail. Of course, I made a fuss of him and praised him highly for his performance. It was of course for me if not for Oscar, good news. Because it proved that Bentley had had some recall training, he knew his name and would come when called. This was a very good start! We clearly had much to look forward to.

Oscar on the other hand, was in a real state, he was very upset. This was all a bit much for him. He was clearly grieving for the gentle dog that he loved. Bruno had always been his safe place. If he and Bruno were in together, Oscar would sleep with his head on Bruno's chest, he couldn't understand where he had gone. In the previous days, he had been sleeping on Bruno's blanket and when awake he had been looking everywhere for him. If the neighbours left the door into their house open, Oscar would walk in looking for Bruno, when he didn't find him he would run out. It was clearly going to take him some time to accept such a big change in his life.

While Oscar was slowly coming round to the idea that there was some other dog in his house, Bentley was making his presence felt in many ways. He decided that our bedroom was, in fact, our shared kennel. He believed that there was a lock up time, that was what he must have been used to at The Dogs Trust, he retired to his bed at 7pm every night only making occasional sorties to find out why we weren't in bed. Of course he had decided that our bed was his bed. That was only a problem when he decided that the wooden bed end was a good place to test his teeth.

There were other items that came to a sad end when he decided to chew them. Two pairs of my slippers, one pair of Margaret's, a sleeve off one of Margaret's coats, any item Bentley found was fair game. As I was writing this a cushion lost it's floral decoration, what a good boy. After all, he could easily have ripped the cushion to shreds, he is clearly showing great restraint, Bentley just wants me to pay attention to him, not this book. Any food in the house was there for him, even if it was ours. Anything on the working top in the kitchen or on the dining table was fair game. Once he even took a piece of toast out of my hand, I wasn't concentrating, I was reading the paper and the toast was very gently plucked from my fingers. All this was transient, not to be worried about. As anybody who has a dog will know these little peccadilloes will pass as your dog matures.

In other ways his conduct in the home was impeccable. There was one little accident when he first arrived he had a little wee in the hall, nerves or excitement no problem. It has never happened again. He has turned out to be an absolute joy of a dog. He only wants to love us and be loved in return. People, dogs, horses, anyone, or any animal I have ever known, are happier when they are loved. It was two days before Bentley barked, we thought that was strange but just waited to see if he barked when he became more confident in his new surroundings. Then he found his voice, a squirrel defied him when we were walking in the woods, it wouldn't come down out of the tree. Bentley certainly let that squirrel know what he thought of its behaviour. Having found his voice Bentley has gone on to show that he is a dog who uses his voice sparingly. He never barks twice if once will do, He doesn't bark at all unless he decides we need to know something that he knows.

On his walks, Bentley likes to range far and wide of the bridal path, but he travels in circles. When whistled or called he invariably comes back at the gallop, from behind. Then he sits looking up at you till you tell him to run on. Then the process will be repeated. We did have a bit of a surprise on our walk one day, when he came racing to me and sat at my feet, with his head upturned, I looked in his mouth and saw a round object. Oh God, I thought it could be a golf ball, please don't let him swallow it. "Give it to me," I said, hopefully holding out my hand. He opened his mouth, dropped the item in my hand and I saw that it was oval, not round. It was an unmarked uncracked pheasant egg. Proving that he, like all our other previous dogs, has a soft mouth.

There was another incident in fact for Bentley it was more of a shock. We, Margaret, Bentley and I were walking along the bridle path on a beautiful sunny day, Bentley had responded well to everything that we had asked of him. He was being as good as gold trotting along beside us as we made our way home. Suddenly around the bend in front of us appeared not one not two but six mounted horses. Bentley was terrified, I don't think he had ever seen one horse never mind six. He ran up the bank next to the path and stood in the trees. Then from his point of view, the situation took a turn for the worse. The lead rider leapt down from her horse, a very stylish dismount, saying, "What a lovely dog, don't worry the horses are all used to dogs". Bentley began to bark hysterically, he must have been thinking what manner of sorcery is this, I see one beast and now it has split into two. By this time I had got hold of his collar and I put his lead on. As I led him away I decided to take him up the stables so that he could learn that horses are no threat to him. In time Bentley might even learn to love horses as much as Margaret and I do.

Many years ago as I mentioned earlier Lucky had a habit of bringing me the present of horse apples. He, as I said, grew out of this habit. Bentley has taken an obsession with manure to a new level. He rolls in it. Or to be fair to him I should say he has been known to roll in it. Afterwards he seems very pleased with himself. He seems unaware that the smell emitting from his lovely coat is almost unbearable. It has been over a week since the last time he did this, so we live in hope that the novelty has worn off for him. We are keeping his special shampoo on hand just in case. He is still a lovely boy.

A more pleasant pastime for Bentley is a swim in the river and when he comes back out of the water he always shakes himself, all over the nearest person, usually me! Then he leans against my leg so my trousers are good and wet. He really is a lovely affectionate dog. A good companion and fast becoming a loyal friend. There is no doubt he is a very fine dog. There are lots of ways that Bentley has of showing affection but one I think is most endearing. When he decides that it is time for us to go for our early morning walk, he wakes me up by getting on the bed beside me. Then he wraps a paw around my arm and puts my thumb in his mouth. If any dog has a more affectionate way of showing his devotion, I have never seen or heard of it. Bentley is a very welcome addition to our family and we are delighted with his contribution to our happy home.

Bentley is a loving caring dog who can't do enough to show how much he thinks of you. If he comes to you he puts his head on your knee, then his feet keep shuffling forward until his chest is resting against your legs. He looks into your face with his most expressive eyes.

Dave with Bentley in 2020

Bentley is a really gentle dog who demonstrates his caring nature at every possible moment. As you will see from the photos in this book, Oscar has warmed to Bentley and now sleeps beside him on the settee. Brandy is totally relaxed around him. It doesn't seem possible in such a short time but Bentley has become a much loved and important member of the family. We are hoping that he will enjoy a long healthy happy life. There will be problems because we understand that Bentley is a very nervous dog. His previous life has made him this way. We feel that love and patience will help him overcome past fears. We have been blessed to have the opportunity to share our lives with another wonderful dog

CHAPTER NINE

Bonnie

… and the other dogs who shared some time with me but weren't mine

As the years have gone by I have known quite a few good dogs who belonged to other people. They ranged from a little Scottie dog who belonged to my godmother. He is one of the only two dogs to have bitten me in more than seventy years, I don't remember his name, but when I was three years old he taught me a lesson for life. I took his ball when he wanted it, he only nipped my finger but I learned to be clear in my intentions and also talk to any dog I was with like an equal. That is why in my opinion only one other dog has ever bitten me. Lovely dog, he never held my indiscretion against me. I visited him many times and he always made me welcome and let me play with his ball. He was a good dog.

The range of dogs led in no particular order to a little black Labrador bitch called Bonnie. Had it not been for my bout of serious ill health, she may have become our dog. What she turned out to be was a great companion for Lucky, she spent every day for six months at our house while her owner was at work, going home with him at night. She was an easy dog to train, I took her on walks with Lucky and the great thing about her was she always understood the word no! It makes life very easy when a dog is tempted to do the wrong thing, like going under a five bar gate into a field where there might be sheep. She always stopped and came back when she heard the word no!! She loved being at our house so much that one Sunday, when she wasn't due to be with us, her owner drove through the village on his way somewhere else. He always had her on the passenger seat of his van with the window open, he slowed as he passed our gate, to wave to me and say something to me, I was in the garden. Bonnie took the opportunity to jump out of the window, jump over our gate and lie down beside Lucky, on the patio. Her owner just laughed and said I will pick her up on the way back.

He got a job in Spain, with a two-year contract in May of 2009, it was decided that we would have Bonnie when he went away. It never happened because I was ill in hospital. Margaret would not have been able to cope with two dogs, so the plan failed. What neither of us could have predicted or anticipated was, that Lucky would die in August of that year. So Bonnie could have come to Margaret. Sadly it just wasn't meant to be. As it happens I have never had two dogs at the same time, for reasons that I explain in the last chapter of this book. Bonnie was a lovely dog and a good companion for a few months but clearly she was never meant to be mine, or ours.

Tiggy

As I say there was no pattern to the way I am remembering the dogs in this chapter. I recall my father and stepmother having a lovely mongrel dog called Tiggy, she was a good-natured dog who always made me welcome when I visited. I remember she once stole the Sunday joint of meat when it had been left to rest on the kitchen table, that was I think the only time she put a foot wrong. They were different times, I think she ran in their big garden but never went for walks due to the constraints placed by the necessity of going to work. Tiggy certainly seemed to enjoy a free-ranging life, sometimes escaping the garden but always returning home.

As a result of one of her excursions around the neighbourhood, Tiggy had a litter of pups and one was kept as a pet for my sister. She called him Tim, he looked for all the world like a stocky border collie, nothing like his mother, probably gaining his appearance from his unknown father. He was black with a white ruff around his neck, white paws and I think there was white on the tip of his tail. Tim was a fun-loving dog who once again I would see on visits. He lived a long life, although sadly he went blind towards the end. Tiggy had another litter in later times and the two pups that were kept were retriever-like black dogs called Mac and Max. I remember they were good fun and liked to chase sticks and balls. But as I didn't spend much time with them that is all I remember of them.

Smokey

My Aunt Betty and Uncle Jim had a wire-haired fox terrier called Smokey. I always enjoyed taking her for walks. She was the only other dog to bite me. Again I have to say it was not her fault. At the age of ten or eleven, I'm not sure which, I had been cast as Joseph in the school nativity play. On the night of the performance, because Uncle Jim and Aunty Betty lived too far away from us to come by bus to see the show it was decided that I would be taken to see them in the car after the show.

Before I continue, I should say that this would be the last time I would ever be cast in any school production. I was waiting in the wings with some members of the cast who were like me, not due to be on stage yet, I was sitting on a form with my staff on the floor at my feet oblivious to everything. In my head, I was, as always roaming the Cumbria fells. That is why I am so ill-educated, learning my lessons was not important to me. Only dogs, horses, sheep and cattle held my attention. Suddenly for some reason, a girl from my class kissed my cheek! My foot jerked as I turned to see who it was. My foot caught my staff which rolled out on to the stage, apparently it sounded like thunder at the back of the hall. The headmaster rushed to berate me. It seems that my lack of care and control of my staff had ruined the play for everyone, I would never have been allowed to be in any other production! I could have cared less. You don't need an education in drama to work with cattle. Having said that the headmaster kept his word.

However, I arrived at my aunt and uncles home in full regalia, white sheet for a robe, a multi-coloured towel on my head and a broom handle for a staff. Also to darken my face, the teachers had applied makeup and to give my appearance realism, they added a false beard. I rushed into the house eager for my aunt and uncle to see my splendid appearance. What resulted was complete pandemonium. Smokey, a dog never heard to bark or become excited, went berserk, barking and snapping, doing all she could to defend her home and family from the monster that had appeared in her home.

Afterwards, when I had divested myself of the sheet, towel and staff. I washed my face and sat on the sofa with Smokey on my knee. I had plasters on two of my fingers. This was a lesson well learned, dogs do not like to be shocked or surprised. I don't think Smokey ever realised that she had bitten me, Nor do I think my aunt and uncle really saw my outfit. I did get the bar of chocolate that they had bought me to say well done for being in the play. We didn't know in the early fifties that chocolate was bad for dogs, so I gave Smokey a piece to show that there were no hard feelings. She really was a lovely affectionate dog.

Jason

I can't write this chapter without mention a lovely Golden Labrador called Jason. He was a pedigree dog, a fine example of the breed. He belonged to my friends Peter and Lynda and he was gentle and affectionate with everyone. His kennel name was Ulysses and he lived up to his two noble

Greek names. There may have been more than just Ulysses on his papers, but I don't recall if there was. I do remember that he was the colour of the Golden Fleece from Greek Mythology, I suspect that was why Peter gave him his name. His welcome when I visited their home still remains in my mind, tail wagging, tongue licking my face he couldn't have treated me better. They later had a lovely Spaniel type dog called Rocky. I can't say little else as I didn't really know him.

Ryan

My father had a lovely white German Shepherd called Ryan. He came from the dogs home, like our dog Bruno he had run wild with a pack for some time before being caught. Unlike Bruno he never lost the urge to run, Ryan also chased buses, a dangerous pastime, for any dog. I can't fully remember what happened to him, I suspect he got away once too often. In those days micro-chipping was not an option so I suspect he made his home with whoever found him next. I hope he enjoyed a happy life because he was a gentle and affectionate dog.

Judy

My sister Christine and her husband Dennis have had some lovely dogs and I will try to remember them all here. There was Judy a happy little mongrel, she was my sister's shadow. Always wanting to make a fuss of people, sadly her life was not long. But she clearly enjoyed the life that she had.

Kym

Then there was a lovely little Alsatian named Kimberley, later shortened to Kym. I say little because she had been operated on for stomach cancer and it stunted her growth. This did not prevent her having eight puppies sired by my sister and her husband's other dog Shep. He was a Lurcher very fast-moving and full of fun between the two of them they produced lovely pups.

Sheba

They took in a stray Sheltie and named her Sheba. She was a lovely dog she used to sit on the window sill looking out like a pot dog. Sheba had a lovely nature and was a very loyal dog. She enjoyed a long and happy life.

Flash, Jess & Molly

Then there was Flash, a really fine Border Collie, lovely black and white markings. He loved his toys but never chewed them. He came from our neighbour's daughter who had not been able to keep him due to moving house. He was a very clever dog quick to learn new things. He was always very fond of me.

As was their other Border Collie, Jess, she was always pleased to see me. Full of fun and she seemed to take great pleasure in destroying Flash's toys after he had taken such care of them. They got on very well and Jess had a very protective nature.

When those two lovely dogs had lived their lives along came delightful Border Collie pup. Her name was Molly, Once again a very clever dog learned things quickly and has a lovely nature. Still full of energy with a zest for life and welcomes us all when we visit.

Anna, Harley and Ivy

Our niece Sandra has dogs that contribute to this chapter, the first Anna a Staffordshire Terrier. I don't know a great deal about her except that once again she had a lovely affectionate nature. She also somehow got a taste for ice cream. Never really got any officially but from time to successfully pinched some.

A while later Sandra and partner Phil got a real Patterdale princess, an absolute joy of a dog called Harley. She was one of our gentle giant Bruno's favourite pals. How much he cared for her is shown in a photo seen in this book. Harley tiny and lovable she brings happiness and joy wherever she goes. Sandra and Phil decided if one Patterdale was good two would be better and brought Ivy into their home. Ivy has a completely different character, she is a loveable rogue who is always into mischief. Her other great delight is playing in water, with all the problems that can bring. Two happy dogs.

Bob & Ted

I cannot end this chapter without mentioning Bob the Jack Russell and his housemate, Ted. These two dogs are great fun and belong to our next-door neighbours Martyn and Jayne. They, in particular Bob, were great pals of our Bruno enjoying many happy walks in the wood together. Bob and Bruno used to tear around like wild things, a joy to behold.

Gyp & Mickey

I am going to mention two dogs who I never met, Gyp and Mickey. Both these dogs played an important part in Margaret's childhood. So they must take their place in this chapter. First Gyp, who was a beautiful Collie cross, a big dog with a gentle nature. Margaret's mum brought Gyp home when she found her being ill-treated by her previous owner. This was before Margaret was born. Gyp repaid Margaret's mum's faith in her by becoming a happy and loyal member of the family. Customers in Margaret's mum and dad's shop offered the opinion that the dog would have to go when the baby was born. "I don't think so" her mum would reply.

She was right as not only was Gyp well behaved but, she also became a loving companion for Margaret while she was growing up.One example of Gyp's loyalty to the family was when Margaret's mum went into the nursing home to give birth to Margaret. She faithfully walked with Margaret's dad without a lead, it was snowing heavily, on the night Margaret was born but Gyp was not deterred by the weather. Dad was coming to visit mother and daughter. When he got to the nursing home he told Gyp to sit and wait while he went inside, this she did. When he came out sometime later there waiting for him was to all intents and purposes a snow dog. Margaret's Dad called Gyp to him, she came, shook herself off and they walked home through the snow together.

As Margaret got older Gyp would let Margaret play, house under the table with her and some of her teddy bears. Gyp also patiently let Margaret dress her up in various items of clothing. Margaret has no idea now why she wanted to dress the dog up. This lovely friendship continued with many happy times, walks and games until Margaret was eleven or twelve years old. At that point unexpectedly because she still seemed well, at the age of fifteen and a half Gyp passed away.

At some point not long after that Margaret's aunt and uncle who had the fruit and vegetable shop, next door got a dog called Mickey. Mickey who was a two-year-old blackish faced and white-bodied Cairn Terrier cross, absolutely adored Margaret and given half a chance would run out of the shop and fly into Margaret's mum and dads shop, to find Margaret. Margaret's aunty was very frustrated by, as she put it, "The dog's behaviour."

Throughout Margaret's teenage years she and Mickey were inseparable. They enjoyed many walks, games and adventures together, very often getting into mischief for which Margaret would be told off. The worst thing that happened was when Mickey jumped in the local river near the weir, Margaret was panicking as she knew there

Margaret's father with Gyp

Mickey

would be trouble if Mickey couldn't get out. With much pleading and cajoling, Margaret managed to get Mickey back on to the bank. There was trouble when she got back with him because of course, he was soaking wet. As her aunt reminded her Mickey was supposed to stay on his lead. Margaret wasn't bothered, she and Mickey continued to play and run free. They went almost everywhere together until when Margaret was twenty she had been to the cinema and came home to find that Mickey had passed away in his sleep. He was ten years old. These two dogs were a really big part of Margaret's very happy childhood.

These dogs who have been there along the way have been just as important in our lives as people who have shared our lives at the same time.

Of course, I can't end this section without mentioning the scores of dogs we have sponsored or supported through the years. These also play a small part in our lives and we eagerly look forward to getting progress updates.

CHAPTER TEN

The reason for writing this book

It has always been in my mind that what these dogs had in common was their spirit. They all thought so much of me and with Rex the second, Lucky and Bruno, they thought much of Margaret as well. My question had been are they all the same dog? Fanciful you may say, but I am not the first to consider it. A very talented author, W. Bruce Cameron wrote a story, the title of this was, *A Dog's Purpose*. Later in 2017, it would be made into a film of the same name. The story revolved around a dog who died, then was born again several times. He was always kept looking for a specific person he had spent part of one of his lives with.

In my case, I believe that with the exception of Bruno who we got from The Dogs Trust when he was four years old, that all the dogs found me straight away, shortly after birth. Or if my premise is right had Bruno found his way back to Margaret, having been her dog when she was a child? Who knows? They all share similar mannerisms and all seem to look through the same eyes. I can never know if this is true but, I believe with all my heart that it is! Having said that we now unexpectedly have Bentley who clearly has so many of Lucky's traits while still having his own personality.

If there was an exception that proves the rule I feel it was, and this may surprise you, the very lovable and gentle Bruno who was the exception. Bruno was so different in so many ways, he found Margaret and I by chance and made us his own. He just filled our lives with his own exciting and new personality. He adored us and right to the end of his life was looking to surprise us. We are so glad that on his journey to find that special someone, he chose us. I wish that we could live long enough to let him find his way back to us. As we are both in our seventies we may have to wait for another lifetime to meet up with him again.

So thank you to all these lovely dogs for letting Margaret and I share their amazing lives. Each one of you taught us so much and brought a fantastic amount of love in our lives. Our thanks also to three very special cats who slipped silently into this story about dogs. First of all, Whiskey, who joined us as a kitten who my brother in law Dennis found under our garden shed and became the most loving companion, not just to us but to Lucky as well. Then Brandy who ran up to Margaret on the street and adopted us for his own. Then Oscar, who came to us from Oldham Cats Home. Two extremely loving cats who enjoyed their time with Bruno and have now adopted Bentley as their own. Each of the pets in our book has made very loving family members and as such will always be deeply missed. We will continue to love the ones who are still with us.

This is a book that has no actual conclusion because it will only end when life itself ends, then who knows, it may start all over again.

I dedicate this verse to all the special dogs who have shared our lives and gone before us.

Your presence we miss
Your memory we treasure
Loving you always
In our hearts forever xx

Anonymous.

At this point I am going to call on an excerpt from a poem by Lord Byron to say perhaps more clearly than I possibly could, how we miss our dogs when they leave us. This is engraved on Boatswain's Statue at Newstead Abbey. It is his ode to his much-loved dog, a Newfoundland called Boatswain.

Near this spot are laid the remains of one

Who possessed Beauty without vanity

Strength without insolence

Courage without ferocity

And all the virtues of man

Without the vices.

The price which would be unmeaning flattery

If inscribed over human ashes

Is but a tribute to the memory of Boatswain

A dog who as born at Newfoundland

May 1803

And died in Newstead Abbey

Nov 1808

In 2016 I wrote a book about our dog Lucky entitled Lucky, A dog's tale. It was well received at the time and I got lots of positive comments about it. It is written as being from Lucky's perspective so puts a 'dog's eye spin on the events of his long and adventure-filled life with us.

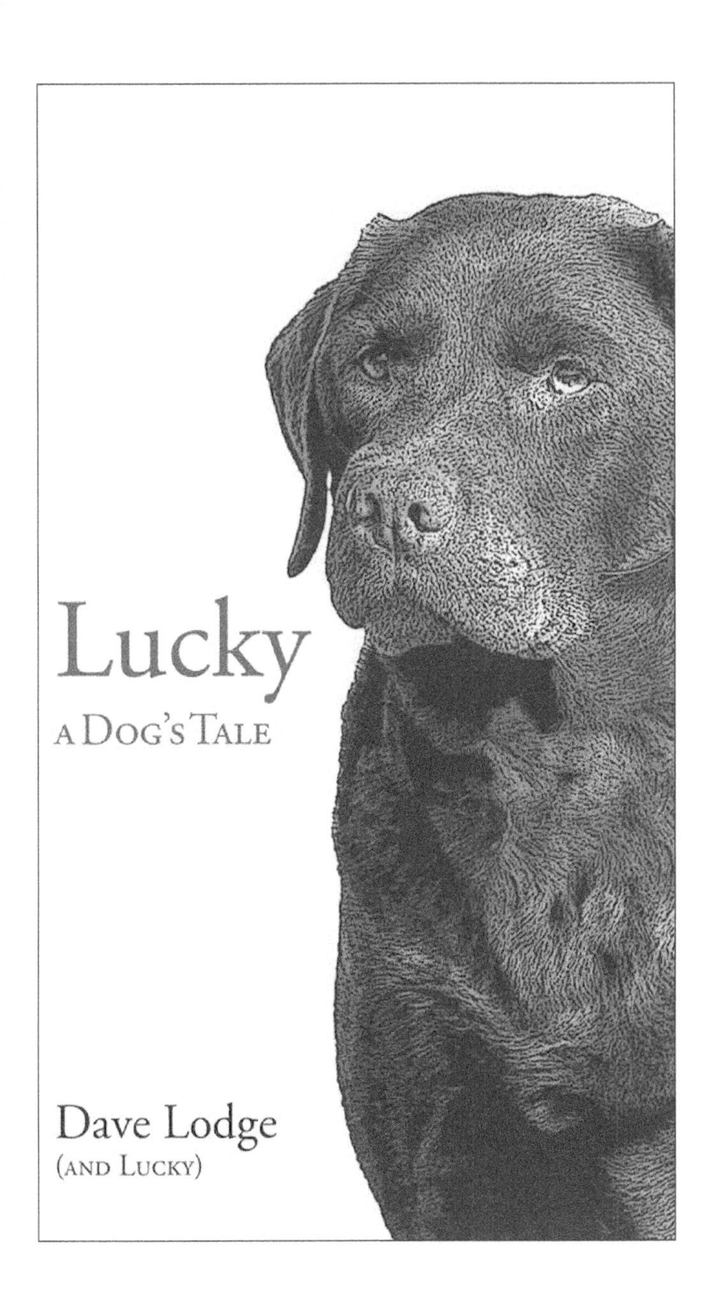
Lucky
A Dog's Tale
Dave Lodge
(and Lucky)

Chapter 1

This is my life story. My name is Lucky, at least that's what everyone calls me! Maybe when you read my story, you'll understand why. There's just one thing I need to tell you just one thing before I continue ... I am a dog.

"What?" I hear you say, "a dog?"

Yes, a dog – a dog can have a life story, can't he? Enough rhetorical questions, I feel a philosophical argument coming on so I will just tell the story, then let you decide the answer for yourselves.

My earliest memory is of finding myself surrounded by others like me – my brothers and sisters; we were all small and vulnerable as we couldn't see where we were or what we were doing. We kept falling over each other and bumping into things ... it was very chaotic. We knew we were related because we could smell a familiar scent. We would all crawl around and find a bigger version of ourselves. It felt warm and safe being beside this bigger version of us and we would lie close, snuggle up and suckle a warm, sweet liquid from her. I'd heard it called 'milk'; it was delicious, and I liked it.

Over the days and weeks that followed, things were changing around me. I began to see my siblings and with this improved vision we even stopped bumping into each other. I also learned that the bigger version of us who cared for us and supplied the lovely milk was our mother. We seemed to be getting better at moving around and as time went by I started to get to know my surroundings and understand that I was different from my siblings, who I was hearing referred to variously as 'pups', 'animals' and 'dogs'.

Unlike my well-proportioned and frisky siblings, I was clumsy and slow. My head was a big as my body, and I had huge feet that made me trip over. This clumsiness caused me many problems, so I wasn't getting as much food as my speedy siblings.

Our pack share space with a couple of large two-legged creatures, who as we grew bigger, spent more and more time with us. This wasn't a pleasant experience, at times as they were very rough when they handled us and would make a lot of noise. One noise was very loud - it was called 'shouting' and because of my clumsiness, it was usually aimed in my direction.

As time went by I recognised many of the sounds I heard and found they were a form of communication although I only understood sounds used by the four-legged creatures like me; our 'yelps' and 'barks' had different pitches to mean different things.

The large two-legged creatures had a very different way of communicating with each other. Their sounds, which at first I thought were just loud noises, turned out to be instructions and commands meaning they wanted us to "sit" "lie down" or "shut up". I slowly began to understand that some of these words were being aimed at me. Sadly as well as the usual commands I heard one of them say,

"Ugly little devil, all head, and feet"

And I knew it was me he was talking about because I wasn't as well liked as the other pups.

My siblings were treated more kindly than me and the Masters, (as the two-legged ones were called), picked them up and cuddled them all the time. I was never picked up and cuddled.

Then came the day that would change my life forever. It was only a few weeks after I was born and I heard one of the Masters saying;

"It's time some of these pups were gone, they're nearly four weeks old".

Then looking in my direction, he said:

"We need to get rid of that ugly one".

"Right," said the other, who picked me up and threw me roughly in to a cardboard box.

I was then plonked inside another even bigger box ... a metal box with windows, wheels and doors.

"What a strange kennel, with a funny smell" I thought.

Suddenly this kennel with wheels made a loud noise unlike any I had heard before; then I felt it moving.

I was whining and crying – terrified as the box on wheels went faster and faster. I tried to get out of the box. I was so scared and couldn't help wetting myself.

"Right!" I heard one of the Masters shout, "That's it; I've had enough, he's useless to us."

I felt the big kennel slow down, and suddenly a rough hand grabbed me. At that point I was sick, the door opened, and I was hurled into the open air, eventually landing with a bump. I slid and stumbled along the ground before eventually coming to a stop.

I just laid there motionless, trying to make sense of what had happened, I was hurt all over and crying pitifully. Eventually, I mustered some strength, staggered to my feet and tried to wander off. I was dizzy and sore, moving aimlessly.

I felt myself being picked up; I struggled and cried in fear. I soon found myself in a yet another kennel on wheels, with a different smell.

My intuition told me I was being held by a female. Her mate was driving the kennel. I was in a panic and trembling, afraid of the unpleasantness that was bound to come next.

So what a surprise when she lifted me up higher so that we were looking into each other's faces and said in a gentle, calming voice,

"Oh you poor little love, don't be frightened, you will be alright now".

She lowered me back down on to her lap; Then I heard the other one speak,

"Let's take him home and get him checked out."

"Home!" I yelped, "Home! I don't want to go!"

Neither of them seemed to be listening, so I repeated myself over and over again.

"What's he yelping about?" asked the male,

"I don't know" replied the female, "I think, he is probably frightened."

I settled down on the female's lap, and I must have fallen asleep because when I stirred I felt warm and comfortable and my nervousness seemed to have subsided. The kennel on wheels had stopped, and the male said:

"Okay Margaret bring him in."

I looked around as Margaret carried me down a path, saying to me

"Look, this will be your garden now and at the end of the path is your new house."

I felt an unfamiliar contentment wash over me, and I resolved to do everything I could to ensure that these two people would want me to stay with them.

Chapter 2

As I settled in my new home, I got used to hearing the two-legged ones call each other by name. The man is called David, and the lady is Margaret. They had a discussion about what to call me. David said,

"I think we should call him Lucky because we are lucky to have him, and he is lucky to be here after being thrown out of a moving car." Margaret agreed.

So, Lucky it was. I soon learned that I was supposed to 'come' when I heard my name, but that doesn't mean that I always did.

At first David & Margaret tried me with various things to eat, but the only thing I could manage was water and milk. Margaret went out and bought some puppy food. She put some in a bowl and it smelled lovely, but I didn't know what to do with it. Then she had a brilliant idea; she sat on the floor, so she was close to me, got a wooden spoon and put some of this stuff on it, holding it out to me. I sniffed and licked at it, it tasted great, and I was able to suck at the spoon which pulled the food into my mouth, I moved it around in my mouth, and it tasted lovely, then I swallowed, and I soon felt full and sleepy and dozed off. Margaret fed me like that for weeks, in fact, for the next sixteen years I would get her to feed me like that, just for fun, every now and again, it was like a special bond that we shared between us.

David took me for a check-up to McDonald's the vets. I didn't like it much – as we went in it smelt of bad, stale, animal smells and there was one particularly horrible smell that I instinctively knew ... the smell of death! I heard a woman crying, her cat who she loved had been put to sleep, and she was going to miss it. I was really frightened and leant against David's leg. After a while we met a nice man called Patrick, David told me he was my vet and would look after me whenever I was poorly. I liked him; David was talking to him about me, and then I had an examination. Patrick gave me an injection, a sharp thing in the back of my neck which made me yelp. David explained to me that it was to protect me against something called Parvo, I didn't know what that was, but I understood it was part of taking care of me. Even though I liked Patrick, I was glad I'd only have to visit him once a year throughout my life. The vets was a place I would have preferred not to go.

While we were there, Patrick told David that I was only about five weeks old and way too young to have left my mother.

"Ah," said Margaret, "that's why he can't eat properly".

Whilst we were there Margaret asked about something called 'castration'. I didn't know what castration was but as David was pulling a wincing face I assumed it probably wasn't good. Patrick told Margaret that it was something responsible owners usually arranged for their dogs, but that because it looked like I was going to grow and grow he wouldn't do it until I was two years old ... after that there'd be no nights out courting for me!

Everything at the new house was wonderful and new, I had important things to do in the garden, I had to play in the bushes, dig up plants and bury bones. I hadn't quite got the idea of the last one. I would dig a hole, put the bone in the hole and then walk away. David would always say, "he doesn't know that he has to cover the bone with soil".

I thought "If I do that I won't be able to find it when I want it". I never did cover the bones up, nor did I ever go back for them. I liked the idea of these bones, but I wasn't sure why I got them.

Life in the new house was great. I wasn't the only four-leg in there, though. There was another creature, she had soft fur, was very fussy and spoke a different language! Her name was Whiskey, and she was a Tortoiseshell cat – she looked lovely, but that didn't stop me chasing her up the stairs. I didn't know it then, but Whiskey would be like a mother to me, and we would become great friends.

Whiskey's story was similar to mine. David had found her under the garden shed, and she was very small and very hungry. He'd brought her into the house, and Margaret fed her chicken. She never grew to be very big, but she grew to be a lovely cat and was active and healthy.

She stayed with David and Margaret; they loved her, and she loved them. She would often jump up on David's knee then get up on his shoulder and go to sleep on his neck. The whole environment seemed just right for a happy life.

David would go off to work every day, and I'd spend my days with Margaret. So when he came home from work at night, I made sure I was waiting at the gate. I'd get up on my hind legs and put my front paws on him as high as they could reach, which was just below his knee and just look up at him. He liked this and always picked me up and made a fuss of me. Of course, as the years went by and I grew I still greeted him in the same way, but my paws would be draped over his shoulders, he couldn't pick me up anymore, but he still made a fuss of me.

One day David and Margaret had gone out and left me to look after the house. I was feeling a bit bored on my own and after having a look around the living room thought I would have a quick chew on the corner of the armchair to pass the time. It was great fun, the stuffing from the chair was flying everywhere. I went from the chair to the sofa and tore it to bits too. I looked for dessert and wandered towards David's recliner, but I was so tired by then I just curled up on it and went to sleep instead.

When David and Margaret returned I jumped down and ran to them with my tail wagging, I was sure they'd be so happy at my hard work. They were looking around the room just shaking their heads in disbelief. I knew they were pleased! I couldn't wait for them to go out again so I could do something equally impressive for them.

The next time they went out I pulled books out of the bookcase and tore them to shreds. Paper and cardboard were everywhere. When David and Margaret came back in, I rushed to them full of excitement; They looked round, saying,

"Well, at least he doesn't do things by half".

Then David said as he was picking up the torn paper,

"You know Margaret it's funny, but it seems he is partial to destroying your things. He tore up your chair and the sofa but left my recliner alone, the only books he has torn up are your Catherine Cookson novels. I think we need to get him something to keep him occupied when we are out".

"Good idea," said Margaret. "If he keeps on the way he is he will destroy the whole house".

Soon I had been given all sorts of things to play with, toys that squeaked, bouncy balls, rubber bones and pulling ropes. The pulling me were my favourite, I would hold my end of the rope in my mouth and try to drag David out of his chair while shaking my head vigorously from side to side, I always won – I have incredibly powerful jaws. I knew he let me win, and he always told me how strong I was. I got stronger and stronger, all the exercise I was getting was doing me good.

For the first time in my life I felt I belonged, I felt part of the family and life was good. There was food whenever I needed it and always fresh water for me to drink.

I was getting plenty of something called 'exercise. Three times a day I'd be taken out for a nice walk. They were only short walks, at first, but as I got bigger they got longer and longer. The only drawback was I had to wear a collar and lead when we went for these walks. I wasn't keen on this and used to jump around and try to get the lead out of Margaret or David's hand.

Going on walks was my precious time with just David and Margaret, we didn't take Whiskey with us, even though I wanted to because she was my companion. Whiskey preferred to be more solitary; she would go off and exercise alone. Having said that we were always pleased to see each other when we got back.

I also found out from listening to Margaret and David that I was part Newfoundland and part Labrador. Apparently, this combination meant that I would grow up a very big dog. Margaret asked David,

"How big?"

He replied, "We will need a saddle for this one."

I did grow to be as enormous as predicted and despite my clumsiness and lolloping size they loved me for who I was, they'd say 'Lucky is just himself, there is no other like him, he is one in a million'. I liked that ... but I never did get the saddle I was promised!

Chapter 3

As the weeks went by and I grew bigger and stronger something new was added to the outings called 'training'. This was very exciting; we went onto a big green space they called a field – they would let me off the lead, and I'd run free. They'd throw a ball for me – the idea was I should catch it in my mouth and take it back to them so that it could be thrown again. Sometimes, to be mischievous, I just kept running around pretending not to hear when they called my name; it was a good game and made me laugh watching Margaret and David running around trying to catch me.

My training was very frustrating at times for David. There were too many distractions, other dogs that I wanted to say hello to, cats that were hiding in the bushes that needed chasing, other dog's balls that I thought I could catch and run after.

Probably the final straw with my behaviour came as David and I came as we were coming back from a walk one evening. I was quite tired as we had been running around for over an hour and I was looking forward to a nice cold drink of water and a lie-down. We were almost home when I saw something that meant there was more fun for me to have.

Squirrels and cats were in my opinion put on this earth for the sole purpose of being chased by me, so when I saw a cat I had to go off in hot pursuit. As I sprang into action, I heard David call me back.

"Ha," I thought, "no chance". He kept shouting, the cat kept running, and so did I. The cat turned down his garden path as I was gaining on it, so I hurtled down the path towards the open back door just as the cat ran through it.

The crafty cat may have thought it had reached safety. He ran in to the living room and jumped on an armchair with a meow of relief. He was suddenly brought back to reality though as a massive black dog jumped on the armchair too. As he jumped three feet in the air in surprise on to the sofa, I followed him. The lady of the house was as surprised by all this as the cat and could only watch in disbelief as the cat sprang onto the dining table then up onto the top of a display cabinet with me in hot pursuit. It was at this point things went wrong for me. The lovely clean tablecloth the lady had placed on the table was sliding under my feet - 'oh-oh' I thought as I landed on the floor with a big thud tangled in the tablecloth surrounded by plates and cutlery on the floor around me,

By this time David had arrived and got hold of me. He was apologising profusely; the lady was saying,

"Just get him out"!

I looked up to see the cat laughing at me. I felt a complete fool. When we got home, David told Margaret what had happened. Then he had to go back and apologise properly (to the lady ... not to the cat I hope).

The lady had been very pleasant and forgiving; she had seen the funny side of the incident, saying, "Not to worry, dogs will chase cats".

I had to be put back on to the lead after this incident for future walks, as David said, this time, we'd been lucky that the lady was so nice, but I couldn't be trusted. The trouble was I was having great fun, and I didn't think I needed to pay attention to David or Margaret. I would soon find out that I was wrong.

One evening after they had taken a long time to catch me David was getting exasperated. I heard him say,

"This is pointless, we can't even get him to come back to us when we're in the garden, so what chance do we have of controlling him in an open space, we need a new plan."

It wasn't long until I found out what the new plan was. David would take me out for my first walk every day an hour earlier; that meant he would have to get up an hour earlier for work. He said to me,

"The thing is Lucky, I'm hoping that there will be fewer distractions for you, then we will see if you can concentrate."

I liked this about him, the way he spoke to me as though he knew I understood him, Margaret spoke to me in the same way, and I was coming to the conclusion that I had found my true home.

I realised on the first morning there was a flaw in David's training plan. We walked onto the field; it was dark – very dark, I am dark, I am jet black. So I thought he won't be able to see me, I smiled as I looked up at him, as he was preparing to take my lead off. David smiled back at me and released me, and I raced away. In a couple of strides, I was at full pace, and I was sure I had disappeared from view. "Ha Ha," I thought "I fooled you", I ran and ran, I was happy to be free.

It was very quiet and dark, and I stopped running in a straight line and began running round in circles, wait I thought it is too quiet, why can't I hear David's voice calling for me? I started to panic and to sniff the ground for my own scent, I picked it up and trotted back the way I had come.

After what seemed like an eternity I saw David's shape loom up out of the darkness, I ran towards him jumping up with excitement shouted 'I thought I had lost you!' although to him, I suppose I was just barking, even so, I knew he understood.

He calmed me down and as we walked along together, he smiled and looked down at me saying, 'I'm not as stupid as you thought am I?' he asked. I knew then that he really did understand me and we were the same.

I suddenly felt an overwhelming feeling that I instinctively knew was love, and I knew it was reciprocated, this was the beginning of the relationship that would last my lifetime. We had become great friends but more than that I realised that we were a family, basically David and Margaret were my mum and dad, and I loved them both. Indeed Margaret would say things like, "Your dad will be home soon". He would say to me, "Your mum is getting your tea ready".

We were a real family now, and Whiskey was like my sister. So I loved her too. Whiskey and I spent a lot of time together when dad and mum were out. This was our quiet time, and I have to say we spent most of it lying on the sofa together asleep. But home is where you relax, isn't it? Life was good and unbelievably it was getting better.

Soon a whole year had passed (that's a human year) and as I had been with David and Margaret for 12 months I had something called a birthday! Because they didn't know the exact date of my birth, they would celebrate it on the day we all got together, 3rd of April. It was a lovely surprise and apparently it would happen every year. It was a great day; they made a fuss of me, and I got gifts – a lovely new ball with a bell in it and some very tasty chewy sticks. Whiskey's birthday was on the 10th of November, and that was a great day too. I'm not sure that Whiskey and I thought about our birthdays coming round, but we liked the fact that we were part of a family.

Chapter 4

I looked forward to my walks, and our training was continuing. David would say to me,

"We are learning from, and about, each other."

That told me that we were equals – amazing! Other dogs I met when we were out told me it was most unusual to be an equal. Usually, dogs were called 'pets' and had a master and or a mistress. Even the ones that were well treated were told what to do. I felt very proud – I was family, and just as important, I was an equal.

On our outings things were going very well, David had endless patience with me. He told me that he hated to shout at anyone or anything so if he wanted me to come to him he would make a whistling sound with his lips.

David would walk along, and I would run ahead. He would whistle, and I ran back to him, then he would let me go on again. We'd change it a bit, and he would whistle so I would still run back to him then bit by bit we would add more things to this repertoire. One of them was 'sit' then 'walk on together', then it was 'sit', and David would walk on, and I would stay, watching, he would then stop, tap the outside of his leg and I would run to him sit again, and then we would walk on again. I wasn't always quick to comply, but as I said David was patient, and we just tried the instruction again until we got it right. Soon things were working well, and my responses were almost instantaneous, although there were times when I forgot if I was following a new scent, which seemed really interesting.

Unfortunately sometimes on our walk we'd run into the odd problem – usually not of our making. For example, there was a Dalmatian that unbeknown to us was also being taken on walks along the route that we used. This dog, unlike others of is breed, was very unpleasant and would fight viciously with any dog that was unfortunate enough to be anywhere in his vicinity. His owners suffered most from his behaviour due to a number of vet's bills they incurred due to the Dalmatians attacks on other dogs.

This dog was about eighteen months older than me and a good size. I was growing fast but I was in no way equipped for the unbelievable ferocity of the first attack when it came.

One day dad and I were out walking; our confidence in each other had grown more and more by this time, and I was probably too far in front of him as I walked through the wood into a clearing. Suddenly without warning, something hit me. It was like being hit by a ton of bricks; I was flung through the air, and I landed with a thump on my back. I was stunned and completely disorientated and given no time to recover. I heard a most terrible noise; I didn't know it was possible to growl, snarl, and bark at the same time – but the large, snapping teeth that were surrounded by black and white spotted skin seemed to have all these sounds emitting from them at the same time.

I was paralysed with fear, and I felt myself being bitten and this monster, was salivating all over me. I couldn't breathe, and I was shaking violently. I could hear shouting. I recognised dad's, but the other must have been the monster's owner. Dad's voice wasn't as loud, and he seemed to be in control. The Dalmatian's owner appeared to be hysterical, as out of control as his dog.

I heard dad say,

"Call your dog off, get hold of him, do something"!

The guy replied,

"You have got to be joking; I can't go near him when he's like this."

Time seemed to stand still, and suddenly the monster let me go. I looked up, and dad had hold of him by its collar. It was still snarling and slavering. In a split second it leapt up in the air, and I thought, it was going to rip dad's throat out! I blinked my eyes and in that second everything was quiet, the Dalmatian was on all four feet standing quietly on the ground, dad's other hand was in its mouth. He took it out and told the Dalmatian's owner to put his lead on, NOW! The guy obeyed, Saying,

"I don't believe it, your hand isn't even scratched, how did you do that"? "I don't know" dad replied, "It's something my Grandda taught me, he told me that when it finds your hand in its mouth, the dog is so surprised, it just doesn't bite you, so I just did it, I was lucky I guess".

The other guy was very chatty now, he didn't understand why his dog was like this, he is lovely at home with the family.

"Maybe", replied dad as he knelt down stroking me, "Just try and avoid us in future".

Dad checked me over and surprisingly I was unhurt, He helped me calm down, and we carried on with our walk. As we walked, he told me some wise words ...

"Remember Lucky empty vessels make the most noise, the more people shout, the less you should be frightened of them, they are only shouting because they are insecure and unsure of themselves. Dogs are the same, and this one was so busy slavering and snarling he didn't manage to break the skin when he bit you. You were more frightened than hurt. There is no shame in being frightened, I get frightened but, we have to try to be brave when we are frightened and then these people have no power over us".

I never forgot what he said, and I never barked except to show that I was happy and I never even threatened to bite anyone. I think I enjoyed life more because of this.

Dad was very fond of saying things which made sense, and he said that he tried to live his life by these sayings. His favourite was,

"It's not how many times you get knocked down; your life will be judged by how many times you get back up".

I have thought about this, and it doesn't always have to be physically knocked down. It can bad things happening in your life, and people look at how you cope with this stuff, and they judge you by that.

Another regular meeting on our walks was with a Weimaraner. This dog would come up as friendly as you like and then suddenly attack me. Again not typical behaviour for the breed. We always seemed to meet him on narrow tracks through the trees so that I couldn't avoid him. He used his sheer size and weight to bowl me over then he would stand with both his front paws on my chest, looking down at me. This apparently was his normal greeting to any dog he met when out walking.

I think I was supposed to be intimidated by this but I was growing fast, very strong and with what I had heard dad saying, I felt I should be able to stand up for myself. With this in mind, I resolved that I would. Sure enough, the next time we met he came hurtling at me, I am not sure what happened next or how I came to do what I did. As he came up on me somehow I ducked under him, grabbed one of his legs and heaved upwards, he spun over and landed on his back. I very slowly put one paw on his chest and looked down at him then turned and walked slowly back to dad.

The owners of the Weimaraner spoke, "He's in shock he won't get up, he is trembling". Dad knelt down beside their dog, and he stroked until it calmed down. It got up and stood to look at me. Then dad said very quietly, "Now you know how all the other people who walked their dogs here have felt for a very long time". He went on to say, "I don't know how Lucky did that, I am sorry he felt it was necessary." We walked away.

I am pleased to say that the Weimaraner and I became good friends and were always glad to see each other when out walking. I wish the same could have been said of the Dalmatian. We just gave each other a wide berth. Sadly I heard that after a particularly vicious attack on another dog he had to be 'put down', I wasn't sure what that meant at the time, but I never saw him again.

One thing I do know is that after my incident with the Weimaraner, I never had another fight with a dog or had a problem with any aggression. Dad said it was because I had a quiet presence, so other dogs knew that I was in control. He said he was always very proud of me, I was always very proud of him.

Another amazing thing that happened around this time. I saw snow for the first time! It was incredible. White flakes were falling from the sky, sticking to the ground. As I watched through the French windows, the snow was getting deeper and deeper. I was very excited – so much so that mum and dad let me out in to the snowy garden. I ran here and there jumping and dancing, pushing my nose into frosty white piles of snow. I was covered in lovely white flakes. I just couldn't believe what this strange cold thing was. I eventually came back in surprised to see that all the snow that had fallen on me had melted, leaving me cold and wet. Dad dried me with a towel, and I lay down in front of the fire. From then on every winter I looked forward to the arrival of snow.

One morning Dad let me off the lead, and I ran ahead as usual. After a short while I heard him whistle so, I turned and ran back and sat down in front of him looking up at his face expectantly. Dad looked down at me, smiled, and said;

"You may be brilliant at understanding what is required when I speak to you or whistle, but what is going to happen when Margaret takes you for a walk? She can't whistle, and she won't shout so we want it to be simple for her to bring you back, don't we? We have two choices ... one, either I can try to teach Margaret how to whistle. Or two, I teach you that you come back to us when I raise my arm, what do you think?"

I continued to look up at him and wagged my tail.

"Yes, that's what I thought," he said,

"Okay, off you go then," I didn't need telling twice, I was off and running across the field in a flash. After I had been running for a while, I thought, "why hasn't he whistled for me to come back?" so I stopped and looked back, dad was standing with one arm up in the air. I thought "oh, that's what he was talking about, I'd better go back."

This went on for a while, but after a bit of practice, we got it just right.

During this time Mum and I were having our midday walks together, but I had to stay attached to the lead as she still didn't know I would come back.

The following weekend Dad said,

"Well Lucky, I think it is time for you to show what we can do, Mum is coming out with us today."

We walked up to the field then he let me off the lead, and I ran on, always looking and listening. I heard dad whistle, and I came back and sat down. Mum was very impressed and made a great fuss of me, patting me and saying that I was a good boy. We did that a couple more times and then dad said,

"Right Margaret, Lucky's going to show you something new."

He sent me off, and I ran for a while and then looked back towards him, hc had raised his arm, so I hurtled back, at full pace. When I got back, mum said, "Marvellous, well done Lucky what a clever boy!"

Dad said to her,

"Where we go on this walk and what we do is up to you now Margaret, saying to me, walk on Lucky."

What fun we had, I would dash ahead, every time I turned round mum's arm would be in the air so back, I would run, being praised every time. I realised that this training had been for all of us when we were out we always enjoyed the time. There was none of the stress and shouting that I saw between some of the other dogs and their humans.

It was around this time that I went to the vets for that 'castration' that dad had winced about when I was a little pup.

The operation almost cost me my life. Patrick the vet had warned that because of my size he'd have to use a greater amount of anaesthetic and that could lead to problems.

He told dad and mum that following the operation, it would be vital that I keep warm at all costs. So when I got back home the central heating was on and I was snuggled under a blanket.

Just after midnight though, I could feel myself slipping away and very nearly died. During the night I had became so cold after coming round from such a heavy anaesthetic that my body had started to shut down.

Dad found me in this distressing state and did what dad does best - he took immediate action!

He got down the floor with me and wrapped the blanket around both of us. He knew his body heat would keep me warm.

Margaret phoned the number for Patrick the vet and told him what was happening. He said that Dad was doing the right thing, there was nothing else that could be done for me. Luckily it worked, and in the morning I was fine. Dad and I were close before this but somehow an even stronger bond was formed that night.

Chapter 5

Of course, there was always fun at home as well, and sometimes I would do things that defied logic, and that would cause comments about me. I remember one incident which caused everybody who saw it including our neighbours Geoff and Val to make sounds of disbelief.

It was my habit to chase anything that moves. I would run and bark at anything to make it run – cats, squirrels and field mice. I thought I was very quick and agile, in the garden I would run towards little birds that came to feed on Mum's bird table, they always flew away before I got to them, sometimes they would walk on the path, I thought I would get them then but no luck, they could take off and fly faster than I could run. One day when Dad and Mum were talking over the fence to Geoff and Val. I was lying at Dad's feet when I saw a bird on the ground, I ran as fast as I could and as it took off to fly, I sprang up into the air, straight up. I rose, and the bird flew into my mouth. I turned in the air and came down on all fours. As I landed I heard Geoff say I don't believe it, and everybody agreed with him, I trotted up to Dad and put the bird down at his feet it lay there for a minute, then fluttered its wings moved around then flew away.

Dad said,

"There you go, the sign of a good gun dog, he has a soft mouth."

Geoff said,

"Probably just luck, we'd never see anything like that again."

Dad said

"Maybe not, but I will prove to you how soft his mouth is".

He went into the house and came back with an egg and a cup. He called me to him, and while everyone was watching, Dad put the egg in my mouth. I stood there just holding the egg. Dad said to Mum

"Just walk down the gate and call Lucky to you."

This she did, and I trotted down the path to her. I got to her and sat down.

"Now," said Dad "ask him for the egg",

she held out her hand, and I let the egg drop into her hand.

"Amazing," then Geoff said "it's probably hard-boiled,"

"OK, give it back to him," said Dad. Mum did, and Dad called me to him, I went straight back to him, and he took the egg from me. Geoff said he didn't think that proved anything. "No," said Dad "but this does."

He tapped the egg on the edge of the cup and broke it.

"Well, well", said the neighbours. Dad replied,

"I told you he had a soft mouth" then made a huge fuss of me "well done Lucky" he whispered, as he stroked my back.

I tried very hard to jump up and catch birds a few times after that, but I never succeeded. It must have been luck.

Right from when I was a puppy I liked to nibble people's ears. At first, I could only do it when they picked me up. As I got older and bigger, I'd do it from all four legs if they were sitting down or I would rise up on my hind legs to show I was pleased to see them and still get their ears that way.

On one occasion, David's sister Christine came to see us, and I nibbled her ear. Mum said "mind your earrings",

Too late – one gold earring got into my mouth, and I swallowed it. This, of course, caused great consternation, not because of the value but because the sharp parts might cause me harm.

Fortunately the next day it was passed out the normal way. They always picked up after me, but this time the pile of poo had a bright shiny addition to it. They carefully picked out the earring, and it was duly given a thorough washing in Dettol and returned to Christine.

I think she wore it after that and why not – it's a well-known fact that Dettol kills 99% of known germs so that earring was probably the cleanest in the world after that. Dad and Mum would often laugh at that memory. I never hurt anybody's ear, and I know everybody liked me doing it.

At other times Margaret and I had games to play, by now, I was starting to think of her as mum. One of our favourites would involve mum standing outside the back door, with me standing beside her, she would tell me to stay, then she would throw our ball up the long garden towards the gate. As she threw it, she'd say, "1-2-3 Go"! I would run and get it and fetch it back, but instead of giving it straight back I would run past mum into the house around the kitchen and back out again before dropping the ball at her feet. This would be repeated over and over again, mum and I would laugh all the time.

Mum always knew when I was getting tired, so she would pick up the ball and put it away. Then get me a bowl of fresh cool water and make herself a cup of tea. Then I would lie at her feet while she sat in her chair and drank it, I usually got a drop of her tea as well.

When dad got home from work mum would tell him about our game, and I would make it clear that I wanted him to play as well, he always did, and we had a routine of having a game before going on our evening walk.

Sometimes I changed the game when I played ball with dad. I added to the fun by not giving the ball back. Instead, I would run in and out of the kitchen, dodge around him, go back into the garden – in and out of the bushes, up and down the path and do this until he caught me or

I decided I would give the ball back. We would chase around until we were both exhausted. This I think was part of being equals, he would always let me make my decisions, that meant I came back to him because I wanted to, not because I was made to, when we played games it was because we both wanted to and both he and mum always knew when I needed to stop.

After all, that running around dad would have a sit-down for a cup of coffee, and I would always get a drink of water and lie down beside him. We would have a special treat; dad would have a digestive biscuit and break it in to four pieces, and share it with me, he never left me out, and he always commented on how gently I took each piece from him. I never snatched anything, two pieces of his favourite biscuit, I felt very special. He said we never have chocolate biscuits because they are not good for you Lucky. Some people have been heard to say that digestive biscuits are not good for dogs, I don't know about that, but dad says all things in moderation, so neither of us ever had a full biscuit and I am always well. I was always full of energy, so after a little while we would go out for our evening walk.

As time went on our walks got longer and more interesting, after we crossed the field we came to a footbridge that passed over a stream, then on to a footpath that led deeper into the countryside. Although dad and mum crossed the footbridge, I discovered that I had an instinctive love of water so I would plunge straight into the stream and just mess about until they called me. Then I would run along the path to catch them up.

The first time we went on that walk I heard dad say that there was a riding school close by and in the afternoon, at about the time we were out walking, the horses were let loose into the fields. "What are horses," I thought, oh boy was I in for a surprise. Suddenly, off to our left we saw a gate open, and about thirty of these huge four-legged animals came hurtling down the slope towards us, then the swung to their left, running down into the valley. I was very excited, and it wasn't often I saw bigger animals than myself. I just turned and ran along the ridge above them, looking down on them as I was running. I thought I could catch them and run with them, but they were so fast, that I couldn't keep up with them.

I heard dad whistle, so I turned and ran back to him. He was still standing where I had left them.

"Well done Lucky, I'm very pleased with you, I was worried that you might try and run down the ridge and not come back when I whistled. Now

I know that I can trust you to be off the lead all the time".

We walked along the ridge in the direction that the horses had gone and after a while, I looked down and saw that they had stopped running and they were eating the grass. They seemed to enjoy it which was strange because I only eat grass when I have an upset stomach and I want to be sick. As we walked along, I saw some other animals that I had never seen before, and dad said they were cows and they were eating the grass as well. They certainly appeared much more sedate than those excitable horses.

These walks were excellent, but little did I know that things were going to get even better.

All I knew was that I was finding life had new things to offer every day.

Also, we had a family friend called Tommy Bruce, he would often come to stay. Tommy was an entertainer, and he and dad were often out in the evening. But when Tommy was in he and I became great pals. He had always had dogs himself, and I enjoyed his company.

Chapter 6

I started hearing a new word 'Holiday' I had no idea what this meant, but I kept being told that I would enjoy it. This word holiday sounded good because, in the normal course of things dad would be missing for at least eight hours of the day, and mum for four. Apparently, this was because they both went to something called work. I didn't think that it affected Whiskey and me very much as we seem to sleep for most of the time they were out.

There was some discussion revolving about a cottage in a little place called 'Bothel', which it seemed was near a slightly bigger place called 'Aspatria'. Mum's, mum had lived there when she was young, and from there we would travel to lots of places around an even bigger place dad called 'Cumbria'. We would go to Keswick, and then there would be trips to the west coast, Allonby

Bay and to dad's sister's caravan at Tangle Wood in Silloth. The beach at Allonby Bay was a place I liked, the only thing I didn't like was the way the sea shouted at me when the tide was coming in, I used to shout back at it, but I wouldn't go into the water. Mum and dad found that very strange as I love swimming and they have trouble keeping me out of lakes, ponds, rivers and streams.

It was always great to spend time there with dad's sister Christine, her husband Dennis and their two dogs Sheba and Flash. The three of us dogs loved to chase sticks together.

Flash who was a border collie, was my great pal and I was very proud of him. One day we were on our way from Bothel to Allonby Bay when a local farmer flagged us down. His sheep were out of the field wandering all over the road. Although Flash had no experience of herding sheep, the farmer asked Dennis if he would let Flash help with rounding up the sheep. This might have seemed a somewhat reckless decision but Flash, under Dennis's control, got the job done, amazing as I say Sheba and I were very proud of him.

One time we stayed at a cottage in Thornthwaite, we enjoyed lots of walks in Winlatter Forrest which was just behind the cottage. Sometimes we'd drive into Keswick, and we would all get a treat there. Needless to say, we had to go in separate cars, four adults and three dogs were too many for one car.

There was another occasion when we were on the reverse journey from Allonby Bay to Bothel. As we were getting close to Bothel, we could see some Grouse chicks on the road. We stopped the cars and Dennis who was driving the lead car got out to see what could be done. Dad got himself in position to make any other cars that approached from either direction aware of the delay.

Three of the chicks had unfortunately been run over and killed before we got there but having moved those to the roadside Dennis was able to reunite the others with their mother in the field.

This act of kindness only served to remind me of why I liked and indeed loved these people.

Over the years we travelled to lots of places in that 'Cumbria' Cockermouth, Maryport, Workington even all the way down to Barrow-in-Furness.

We would often go over to another lovely place called the Eden Valley.

We'd head down the A686 running down past Penrith, Edenhall towards Langwathby, where we would turn left on to the B6412 and head deep in to the Eden Valley. On the way we'd pass through places like Winskill, Great Salkeld, Little Salkeld and the hills of Long Meg and her Daughters to their right with Salkeld Dykes and Lazonby Fell to their left. We'd continue on through Glassonby, Lazonby then over the Eden Bridge and up the hill to Kirkoswald and past the church on the right where dad was christened many many years ago.

At Featherstone Hall we had a choice - turn right and sharp left, or as we usually did, bear left past Lacy's garage over the small bridge past The Crown and Black Bull pubs. The small square where the Post Office used to be on the left, turning right up to the left just after The Featherstone Arms.

I know that's an awful lot of information for a dog to remember, but this was dad's favourite road in all the world, and he'd always give a running commentary about when we drive along it. Mum likes this journey too and the places around it. It was soon etched onto my doggy memory (just in case I had to get home by myself sometime!)

We'd always go that way because dad's Auntie Effie and Uncle Peter used to live there and he liked to think of them as he drove to his home village. After we passed the houses on the left at the top of the hill, we would go straight on across the T-junction, following the road down to Renwick.

Chapter 7

One day they didn't go to work and started putting things in the car. Mum said, "Come on Lucky, we are going on holiday".

Dad had left the back of our estate car open, so I ran out and jumped in, not even stopping to say goodbye to Whiskey. She was staying home this time, but Geoff and Val from next door would make sure she'd be well looked after. Dad closed the tailgate and off we went. I remained standing, dad looked in the mirror and saw me and told me to lie down and relax. I did, and after a while, I fell asleep.

I woke up when the car stopped, and dad let me out, putting my collar and lead on. Then he poured water from a bottle into a bowl, and I had a drink. I was glad of it because my mouth was dry from being asleep. Dad said,

"Right it's time for a little walk to stretch our legs"

I looked around as we walked as there were lots of cars parked near us, I wondered why. Dad told me we had parked on somewhere called 'motorway services', Apparently this was a place where humans had a break from driving their metal kennels and enjoyed walkies too.

As we walked, I could hear the sound of traffic moving, dad who always talked to me when we walked said,

"The motorway is busy today with lots of cars".

We climbed a grassy hill and then went over a style into a small wood with a trail leading through it. When we got on the trail dad took my lead off so I could be as free as he was and I trotted on, sniffing at all the strange new smells.

As I walked along I stopped and cocked my leg and 'marked the territory', other passing dogs would know I had been there before them. To make doubly sure I squatted down and emptied my bowels too. As always dad had a little bag ready for this purpose in his pocket. He picked it up and tied up the bag so we could take it back with us. He'd say,

"I wouldn't like to step in that and neither would anyone else".

The trail took us to the far side of the wood where there was a wire fence running along the edge. Through the fence, I could see some fluffy animals eating grass. I moved to the fence and was tempted to go under it, but I heard dads' voice say,

"No Lucky! Those are sheep, and they don't bother us, so we don't bother them, never chase them, or go near them".

I looked up at him, and we walked back the way we had come, I liked the way he spoke to me quiet and patient in everything he said. I followed him happily back to the car.

Mum was already pouring water into my bowl as we got there. She rubbed my head and asked me if I enjoyed my walk. I wagged my tail to show her I had. Dad said

"Lucky did very well, we saw some sheep on the walk, but he made no attempt to chase them". "very good," said mum.

As we drove off I lay down thinking, if this is a holiday I think I'm going to like it.

While I was asleep, we turned off the Motorway and went on to the smaller country roads. We turned left heading down the A66 towards Keswick, passing Penrith cattle market on the right then The Rheghed Centre on the left. There were many interesting places that we passed as we travelled along. Greystoke, made famous by Edgar Rice Burroughs in 1912 through the pages of his book 'Tarzan of the Apes'. You see it's amazing the things a dog can pick up if he listens to the people around him. After a while, we would turn on to the A591 heading down past Skiddaw and go round the back of Bassenthwaite Lake following the road to Bothel to the cottage.

When I woke up I could smell water, not like the water mum puts in my bowl, this was a strong, intense smell of water mixed with fresh air and trees! I looked out of the rear window, as we drove past lots of trees. Through the trees, I could see a large expanse of water. I started to bark excitedly not really knowing why. Mum and dad laughed saying,

"Settle down Lucky, it's all right - that's Bassenthwaite Lake, we're going to take you there tomorrow".

I continued to bark, I always liked to have the last word, dad laughed again saying, pipe down, we should have called you 'last word Harry'. I stopped barking and laid down. It wasn't long before the car came to a stop. Dad opened the boot and said,

"It's OK Lucky this is our holiday cottage."

I jumped out and ran straight through the open door.

I followed mum via the lounge, through the kitchen and into a small back yard with some steps leading to a garden. Mum went up the steps,

"Come on Lucky, see the lovely garden that we have here for you".

I ran up the steps to find a long stretch of grass with a fence and a gate at the end. I loved it, and I ran round in circles only stopping to cock my leg and have a pee against the fence.

When I looked round, I saw that mum had gone down the steps and back into the house, just as dad was putting a bowl of water on the floor for me, I went to it and drank gratefully.

As I was drinking, mum said

"I'll put the kettle on and make a brew."

"Right," said dad, "I'll bring the bags in and get them upstairs".

I followed him as he headed out to the car and traipsed backwards and forwards in and out of the house. There was something important I could help with - important things such as my lead, my ball, my bone, and not forgetting my squeaky toy (I must admit I caused a few delays with that one. I couldn't help it, the thing kept talking to me!).

When he took the bags upstairs, I went up and down the stairs with him. The stairs were very steep, they didn't bother me then, but as the years went by they got harder and harder to climb until after about eleven years I stopped climbing them. I will tell you about that later.

After we'd finished unpacking dad and I went through to the kitchen and found that mum had made us something to eat. It was a lovely day, so we ate outside in the garden. I thought it best to feed myself today as I didn't think mum would appreciate her food going cold. There's a time and a place for getting my own way.

There was an elderly chap living next door, and he spoke to us over the fence while we were eating.

"Yon's a big dog," he said, "Do ee bite"?

I got up and walked over to the fence and put my head over it while wagging my tail. The senior man stroked my head.

"No Lawrence, he doesn't bite, his name is Lucky" said Dad.

I liked him, mum and dad said he had lived in that house all his life.

From then on Lawrence always made a fuss of me and we remained friends for many years. Mum said she very often couldn't understand a word Lawrence said. Dad said it was a local dialect and not very different to the one he grew up hearing and speaking in a village not too far away.

After tea, we went for a walk round the village.

"So this is Bothel," I thought. It was very quiet, and I liked it, I'd come to know the place very well over the coming years as we went to stay there two or three times a year.

The next day we got up early, had our breakfast then we went out to the car. I saw that dad was carrying a couple of towels. Usually, these were for if it rained when we were out walking. Strange I thought, the sun is shining and no sign of rain. Where I wondered as we got in the car can we be going?

I didn't have to wait long because after driving for about ten minutes I smelt that lovely smell from yesterday, water. I started shouting which I knew they thought of as barking, but I wanted them to stop.

"It's all right Lucky," said dad, "I'm just parking the car then you can go down the slope in front of us and see what you think of Bassenthwaite Lake". This would become my all time favourite place.

Just before dad opened the car, mum said,

"what if he struggles to swim"?

"No problem," said dad, (he was a very strong open water swimmer and had competed in triathlons), "If it comes to it I'll break all the rules and go in and get him".

Then he opened the door, and I ran down the slope and jumped into the lake. I swam in a straight line across the lake, then turned and swam back.

As I climbed out of the water and shook myself, I saw mum and dad waiting on the bank, smiling with towels in their hands. Mum said my swimming was the most marvellous thing she had ever seen,

I felt very proud. Then we walked along the side of the lake, dad picked up a stick and threw it as far out across the lake as he could, and I would run down into the water then swim out, get the stick and bring it back for him, after doing this several times I would get tired so they would call it a day. I'd still go to the water's edge trying to show that I wasn't tired, but they knew. We would get back to the cottage, very hungry tired and happy. After eating, I usually lay down and went to sleep.

When I woke up, it would be time for our evening walk, through the lanes around the village. No matter where we went our days always started with a trip to Bassenthwaite Lake, and I would swim, it was my holiday, and I loved every minute of it. Even if it poured with rain somehow, there were always dry towels for me, and no matter what the weather I never heard them say that we would not be going to the lake or for a walk, we always went. When we had been for my morning swim, and I was dry and back in the car, mum would say where we would be going that day.

One day she suggested we go to the Solway Firth, Allonby Bay.

"OK why not, let's see what Lucky thinks of the sea," said dad.

Great, I thought, something new, I had no idea where we were going, but I always trusted that I'd have a good time when we got there.

After a short journey along the coast road, we arrived at Allonby Bay. We pulled on to a car park behind what dad said were sand dunes, and we got out of the car. We walked up and over the top of the sand dunes, I could smell something different in the air. I would later know that it was salt carried on the breeze from the sea water. I'll never forget how excited I was to see the sea lapping against the shore. I raced into the water biting at the waves and barking wildly. It was great day, we walked along the beach, I chased sticks and had lots of fun.

Over the following years we went there often, some days were calm when the sun shone, other days in bad weather when the waves went very high and made a lot of noise when they crashed onto the beach. It was as if the sea was shouting at me and it frightened me so I would shout back at it. In future times I would not go in the sea, I just played on the beach.

On one of these trips to Allonby Bay I had a frightening incident, and I have to say it was all my own fault. By now I was completely trusted, and except for this one occasion, I always did what was asked of me (you notice I say asked because dad always treated as an equal).

On this particular day, we'd walked about half a mile along the beach, then, because the tide was coming in, we climbed over the sand dunes at the point we'd got to and came on to a stretch of grassland that we hadn't walked along before. I was wandering along just ahead of mum and dad as I usually did when I saw what I thought was a small lake ahead of me. I took off like a rocket running full pelt towards this great place to swim. I heard dad's voice calling to me to stop and come back, but I thought "I'm in now", so I ignored him. Big mistake! I was going so fast that I was half way across before I stopped. I knew straight away that I was in trouble, it wasn't water it was deep thick mud, worse than that it smelled terrible, it smelled like the filling station where we stopped for petrol and oil.

I tried to get out but I couldn't move my legs, and I was sinking. I was stuck, and it was awful, I was very frightened. Dad was a very powerful man with strong legs and arms from triathlon training so, with no hesitation he broke the rule about letting dogs fend for themselves and ran in after me, the mud was up to his knees, but he got to me. Then he reached down into the mud underneath me and picked me up. Then with a tremendous effort, he carried me to the firm ground. That was very lucky he said, my feet were on the solid ground otherwise we were both sunk.

By now the tide was in so, we walked me back to the sea, and dad and I went in to wash as much of the oily mud off as we could. They were worried about me as they knew about my sensitive skin. I had suffered from eczema throughout my life.

As we walked sedately back to the car, dad said to me,

"You've got to start thinking before you go running headlong into things", he always amazed me by talking to me as though he knew I understood every word he said. Other humans didn't talk to their dogs the way dad spoke to me, and they just didn't seem to have the same faith in their pets as he had in me.

When we got back to the cottage, they gave me a good wash down in the shower with my special shampoo. When I was dry, they put my special skin cream on. As it happened, I didn't suffer any ill effects from my stressful experience.

Sometimes on the way back from the seaside we'd call in for lunch at the Trout Hotel in Cockermouth. Being a clever dog that liked to listen to my knowledgeable dad I'd heard him say a two-leg called Wordsworth had once lived in Cockermouth - he liked to wander around like a daffodil apparently, and his house had been just a few yards away from the hotel. Also, a famous singer called Bing Crosby used to stay at The Trout Hotel when he came over for the fishing. These things weren't really of much interest to me, of course, the main thing about the place for me was that the grounds went down to the river, so more swimming for me!

Sometimes dad's sister Christine and her husband Dennis would pop along to the cottage for a visit. They would bring their dogs Sheba and Flash with them. I liked Christine, Dennis and the dogs, and we rubbed along together very well, so we always had a good time. Having said that Flash was younger than Sheba and I and sometimes he would want to mess about when we were trying to sleep. If he did, I told him off; he was a good lad at heart, so he always listened to me and go off and do something else, leaving Sheba and me to have a kip.

It was around this time that Sheba passed away. I know Flash missed her so much. I was sorry she was gone, she and I had been great pals. It was probably around a year later when another dog came to live with them – a Border Collie called Jess. The three of us got on very well together.

One of the other trips we would make was to the village dad came from. We would visit the farm where dad's childhood friend Robert lived with his wife Linda and their son Edward. I enjoyed myself there, and they had a Labrador called Marple. Marple and I would have great fun running round the farmyard chasing each other.

Sometimes we'd walk through the village round the surrounding lanes out towards another village called Croglin, as we walked he would tell mum and me about his childhood days. I could not have been happier, and I think they both knew it. All in all these holidays were wonderful, and I really enjoyed them. Mind you for me even when we were at home every day was a holiday.

Chapter 8

My relationship with mum and dad was different from the one that Whiskey had with them, because, for her own reasons Whiskey stayed at home and did her own thing, I went nearly everywhere with them, having said that the four of us made a really happy family.

David and Margaret's best friends, Peter and Lynda Leonard often came to our house, They were very nice people, and I liked them, and I could tell that they liked me.

I would stay with them if Margaret and David needed to go away on their own; this would happen once or maybe twice every year. I quite often had a day or so with them, but I occasionally stayed for a week. I really enjoyed being with them, they always made me feel welcome and treated me so well. If I hadn't had dad and mum in my life, I would have happily lived with them all the time. They gave me a real home from home on these occasions, and Lynda even gave me old shoes to chew.

Peter seemed to be very fond of calling me "Stupid Dog"! This was because he instructed me in a different way than I was used to. I didn't always pick up on what he was saying, so he must have thought that I wasn't very bright. However he said it in an affectionate way, so it didn't stop us having some great walks together, we just got on in a different way.

There was one unfortunate incident that happened one time I was staying at their house. It involved their garden pond, and some fish that I heard were called Coy carp. I went out in the back garden on the first day of my stay when I reached the corner of the house I turned left into the actual garden and was delighted with what I saw – a fish pond! Without hesitation, I ran forward and jumped in for a swim (I do like a good swim). There was an almighty SPLASH. Water flew up in the air, and the Coy carp were going in every direction. Not one of my better decisions – this time I really had been a stupid dog. I was in big trouble and needed cleaning up.

I decided that in future the Coy carp could have that pond. Peter and Lynda forgave me, but I knew they weren't pleased. Just another case of me acting without thinking, again! A habit I have worked very hard on correcting. However in spite of the mistakes I made from time to time, even when things went wrong, life was still all right.

Despite the supply of chewy old shoes I was always pleased to see dad and mum when they returned and would I jump in the car without so much as a 'by your leave' to Peter and Lynda. Nevertheless, I loved them lots and missed them when they later went to live in Spain.

One lovely warm summer day dad and I were out walking along a footpath through the woods, he was wearing shorts and a T-shirt which would later prove to be a mistake. I was off the lead as usual when we saw some youths poking sticks in a hole under the roots of a tree, just as we were coming up to them they dropped the sticks and ran off.

As we walk past I suddenly felt as though I was being stabbed with thousands of needles, I was spinning like a top trying to bite the buzzing things, and ; perhaps know dad was trying to help me but I was almost blind with pain. The pain became too much, so I just turned and ran all the way home, I seemed to keep on being stung all the way. Dad had no chance of keeping up with me, when I got home mum was very worried and asked me where dad was, I couldn't tell her, so she ran out to look for him.

After a while they came back together, dad came in the house and made a fuss of me and told me it was all right, I had been stung by something called wasps. It turned out that his legs and arms had been stung, but he had walked not run, knowing that I would go home. He told us about the time as little boy that he had been stung by wasps all over his face and neck, he said his grandma had put dolly blue all over the stings. Since then he said wasps were no problem to him although, if he had been wearing trousers he wouldn't have got his legs stung.

"Anyway" he said, "Off we go again, we are going to enjoy our walk."

Mum came with us we went back and followed the same footpath.

After a while we were getting back to where the wasps had stung me, so I hung back, I didn't want to go near the place again. Dad stopped turned and spoke to me,

"It's OK Lucky the wasps have gone now they will make another nest somewhere, and we like this walk so we have to get past here or it will spoil the walk".

While he was talking, I suddenly noticed that we had walked past the place where we had been stung and nothing had happened to us. I turned and passed again just to be sure, then I turned and followed mum and dad. I was never stung again but, I never forgot thc experience.

We spent many happy years at the place we called home, and I thought things would never change. Then one day in 2002 mum got a phone call and ran out suddenly, and I didn't know why that was. Dad had had a serious accident, and he had to stay away for a while to get better. Eventually, he came home on two things called crutches and for several weeks he was unable to go out for walks with me. Mum took me but, I couldn't wait to get home, it was no fun without dad. From then on whenever we went out again he leant heavily on a stick and couldn't go far. He'd been told that he'd never be fit for work again and things would never be the same. On the plus side, we were still good companions who took care of each other plus it meant that dad was home all the time and we went everywhere together.

We still went away to the cottage and of course I would enjoy many more trips to Bassenthwaite Lake, and happy, lazy afternoons in the garden at the the cottage in Bothel. Of course, we still made the trips out to Renwick in the Eden Valley to see Robert and Linda, but we didn't go for long walks anymore. Dad was in constant pain, but he still took me out letting me mooch around, although I never wandered too far from him. I was slowing down myself, not running blindly after things when I did as a pup, I'd started just watching cats and squirrels not feeling the inclination to chase them anymore.

By now we had all slowed down our pace of life. After all, I was nearly eleven years old. Some people would be heard to mutter:

"What a big dog, they don't usually live past eight or nine years of age". Dad said

"We don't listen to that we just live every day and enjoy it",

So we did. Even Whiskey was slowing down; we weren't entirely sure how old she was, (you know how ladies can be about their age), she wouldn't even tell me. But she was probably at least two years older than me.

The first thing we noticed was that she didn't see as well as she had. This meant she stopped climbing trees in the garden, and never left the garden, content to wander in and out of the flower beds. If the sun was warm, she'd lie down and go to sleep on the garden bench. Thc days when we chased each other around were gone. I liked to be with her so if she lay down and went to sleep I would lie down close to her and we would both have a nap.

We were spending more and more time up in Cumbria; the big difference was that I found the stairs difficult so instead of going up to the bedroom at night, I slept downstairs. Getting up the steps to the garden at the back wasn't easy, so mum and dad started to talk about making changes. Dad couldn't get upstairs very easily either because of his leg problems so they decided we would give up the cottage and move to a more suitable location. It was a sad occasion when we closed the door of the cottage for the last time.

The place we chose to go to gave us a couple of very happy years, and as it wasn't too far from Bothel, we could still call on Lawrence the elderly chap who lived next door at the cottage. Unfortunately, he wasn't getting any younger, and he was suffering poor health.

By now dad and mum had found a nice Holiday Lodge to stay in. It was a wooden bungalow with a railed veranda which we would sit out on in the evenings. Located on the edge of Skiddaw View Caravan Park it was in a lovely location. It had two bedrooms so Christine, Dennis and their dogs could still come and stay with us. It became home from home just like the cottage had been. We were still able to have our trips out, but our trips to Bassenthwaite Lake were becoming fewer. Although I still loved to swim, because I had arthritic hips I would take a couple of days to recover from my exertions. Eventually, we just stopped going; I missed it, but I knew it was the right decision.

Around this time we had a very sudden and for me an unexpected shock. This was a very sad event and made a big change to our lives, after being very poorly one day Whiskey just lay down and died during the night. Mum and dad were very upset, and so was I, Whiskey was part of our family, and we missed her. She was buried in Christine and Dennis's garden. I wondered why she wasn't buried in our garden, but I soon found out.

One day we packed everything up, and I heard David and Margaret say that we were moving house. Two of our friends Roy and his wife Paula, arrived with a big van and a lot of our stuff was packed in it. When it was full, we got in the car, and Roy drove the van with Paula in the passenger seat. Imagine my surprise and delight when we reached our destination, Renwick the village where dad was born and brought up.

We would be making a new home there, living in a converted barn. We all loved our surroundings, and new people were coming to call, and they all seemed to like me. We settled into a new routine, with walks, a complete change of scene and tempo, and we were all very happy. We all missed Whiskey and wished that she could still have been with us.

Chapter 9

One of the first big changes to our routine came about almost as soon as we moved in. Dad had grown up working with cows, so when he got settled back into the village, he asked Robert if he could do anything to help with his cattle. Robert said he could give a try and feed them in the Low Yard. Dad was delighted because he had spent the last couple of years with people telling him he wasn't able to do anything. He knew he was slow and that he had reached retirement age but just wanted to feel useful once more.

The Low Yard was about five minutes hobble away from our front gate with Dad leaning on his stick. In his prime, dad would have covered the distance in a few seconds, but now he was just pleased to take his time and have something to do.

The new routine involved dad getting up at 5.30am leaving mum asleep in bed and coming downstairs to me. I slept downstairs in front of the fire. Dad would open the front door, and I would wander into the garden and relieve myself. When we went back in he would make a slice of toast and a cup of coffee, we always shared the toast. After his drink, dad would go and tend to the cows, and I'd stay with mum. He didn't think it was a good idea for me to be around cattle in a closed environment when I hadn't grown up around them.

Even though dad was a bit of a slowcoach Robert said he was good with the cattle, even when they were calving they were comfortable having him around. Dad's quiet ways always had a calming influence. It probably took him about an hour longer to feed the cattle than it would have taken Robert, but he enjoyed it, and always said it was worth the extra pain he suffered while doing it.

When he'd get back home, I'd be waiting at the door for him, and he would take me out for a short walk. We were usually back by about 8.30am, and dad would make mum some breakfast. While he was doing that mum would come downstairs and join us. She always fed the wild birds in the garden before coming back in and having her breakfast.

Then mum and dad would sit down listening to the wireless, chatting and reading. Dad's a bit of an author and would often work on his latest book. Life was good for all of us, and we were relaxed and content.

One of the things that dad enjoyed was going to the cattle markets with Robert. They went on a Monday and Wednesday to either Penrith or Carlisle. The trip to Penrith would be along the roads I knew well going out through Kirkoswald, KO as we knew it. Then we would go over the River Eden Bridge and out through Lazenby.

Going to Carlisle was a new experience taking us through and past lots of places that I had never seen before. We went out through Croglin on the B6413 by Newbiggin, Cumrew, Cumrew Fell, cutting across from Castle Carrock to the A69 over Warwick Bridge on though into Carlisle. For a man who spent so many years away from home, working away dad certainly knew his way around. Of course, he walked everywhere when he was young, and you learn a lot about an area when you are on foot. As he said he very often didn't know what a road was called, but he knew where it went. One day we even went to a place called Brampton, I never knew why we went there, but I always enjoyed the trips out.

Sometimes we went out of the village and turned on to the A686 to see friends in Gamblesby and Melmerby. On other occasions, we went out to the right up by Hartside Heights and Gilderdale Forest on the same road to see friends in Alston.

A trip dad and Robert always enjoyed because of their mutual love of horses, was a drive out to Hexham race course. We would go out on the A686 past Alston Ninebanks, Whitfield, Allen Banks and Starward Gorge, turning on to B6305 at Langly, past West Dipton Burn to Hexham.

Every day was an adventure, and I was sharing dad's trip down memory lane.

One day a few weeks after we had moved into our new home I thought a tornado had hit the house, a whirling dervish in the form of a black Labrador bitch called Bonnie had come to visit. Bonnie was the pet of Chris, a friend of dad and mum he was an electrician and it had been decided that sometimes, more often than not, in fact, he would leave Bonnie with us while he went to work.

Bonnie was lots of fun and very lively, sometimes too lively for a venerable 13-year-old like me. Somehow she always knew when I was getting tired. We spent the next two years sharing our walks with Bonnie and helping dad to train her for his friend. Bonnie was a clever dog, and she instinctively understood the word 'no'. She concentrated better than I did at the same age. Dad was kind enough to say she took her example from me and that I was a big help in getting her to understand his instructions. These were great days so when dad told me that his friend Chris was emigrating to Spain and that Bonnie would be coming to live with us I was very pleased.

As happy as I was I had no way of knowing that this idyllic life was coming to an end, I would be parted from dad and mum, and I would have to leave our lovely home, and I never saw Bonnie again. But I am getting ahead of myself we had many happy days, weeks and months still in front of us, friends of many years standing would be coming to visit and stay with us. Roy and Paula, who helped us move, Joan and Pat, Dave and Anne who always brought their dog Candy with them, even Peter and Lynda who now lived in Spain came to see us. These were indeed the best of times.

I told you early in the book about how much I loved snow, but nothing could have prepared me for snow in the Eden Valley. Dad had talked about being trapped in the village in the forties and fifties during the winter, but the first morning I saw it I was amazed.

When dad opened the front door, the snow fell inside. I looked out, and the snow was higher than our garden wall. He had to get a shovel and clear a path to the gate. There was only one road running through the village, and it was full of snow. Dad, of course, had to get to the Low Yard which was even more of a struggle than usual for him to get there. It took him a long time, but he made it after all cattle need feed, come rain or snow.

A little later a farmer from the far end of the village drove down in his big tractor, and this flattened the snow. Making it hard packed. I was pleased about this because it also meant that dad and I could still have our walk later.

The flattened snow had it's own problems because when the temperature dropped the snow would freeze and it became very slippery underfoot. Still, this is a small price to pay for living in, as dad always called it 'Gods own country'. It was the best of places.

In spring and summer the rich brown soil freshly ploughed, was so different from the soil in other places. The crops and foliage so much greener and you would have to be an artist to describe the changing colours in autumn. If you are lucky enough to live any part of your life in the Eden Valley then, you truly have been blessed by God.

However, it seems nothing in life is meant to last forever and our days in paradise were coming to an end.

The day things began to change forever began in the usual way. Because dad had a great sense of responsibility, he always made sure he did the things that should be done, without fail.

I never once saw him fail to do the right thing so although I had noticed for a few days things were not right with him I couldn't have anticipated what was to come. It was nothing specific, maybe more pain, the pain and worry were clearly etched on his face.

Dad was up at 5.30am just as he always did, I went in the garden, as usual, then we had our toast, dad had his coffee and then went to see to the cattle as normal. At this time mum was still asleep in bed, so all was as it should be.

As usual, dad arrived back from feeding the cattle and took me for my short walk. The change to our routine started when we returned. Mum was up and dressed, and she had already had her breakfast.

I couldn't understand why but on this morning they just kept moving around. Dad started putting few things in the car. When he had finished, dad came and got me into the car as I couldn't jump in with a single bound as I did in my youth. Mum came out of the house and got in the car too then we set off. I thought it was just another trip like so many we had taken before, so I lay down.

We drove slowly out of the village. When we got to the top of the hill, dad stopped, paused and looked down on the village behind us, saying to mum,

"I don't know if I'll ever be able to come back here again".

"Of course you will" mum replied, "They'll sort you out, and we will be back in a week or so".

"Maybe" dad replied, "I'm not so surc".

They sounded so sad, and this was not like them. The only time I had sensed sadness like this was when Whiskey died. Then I fell asleep and apart from them stopping for one comfort break we didn't stop until I found we had arrived in Manchester outside our friends Joan and Pat's house.

Chapter 10

Joan and Pat are old friends of ours; I mentioned them earlier when the came to stay in Renwick with us. Joan was one of the first people to see me after mum and dad got me. They had also been next door neighbours before I came along I was always pleased to see them. One of my earliest friends had been their dog, a Rottweiler called Rocky, sadly Rocky was no longer with us.

Before we went into the house, dad took me for a quick walk, when we came back, we went into the kitchen, and I had a drink of water. Mum had given Joan and Pat a carrier bag which contained my bowls and my food; there was enough for week mum said. After sitting and talking with Joan and Pat for a while mum and dad got up saying we will be back to see you after the examination. They went out of the house leaving me behind. I barked and complained, but Joan and Pat were kind making a fuss of me. Then Pat said,

"Don't worry Lucky your mum and dad will be back soon".

I settled down and waited. Several days passed, Joan took me out for walks, but always on the lead, I watched and waited, but there was no sign of mum and dad returning.

Then after a week had passed by suddenly a knock on the door. It was mum and dad, and I was very excited and pleased to see them. Dad took me straight out for a walk. I could see he was struggling and leaning heavily on his stick. He looked very sad, and I didn't know how to cheer him up. He talked to me all the time,

"Lucky you are a wonderful dog, you have been a loving and loyal companion, I am so sad that I may not see you again".

I was so happy to see him but confused by what he said. Before we got back to the house, he said,

"I have loved you and cared for you just as I would have if you had been my son".

We went back into the house, and both dad and mum made a fuss of me, then they left.

That would be the last time I ever saw dad.

A few days later mum came and picked me up, Christine's husband Dennis was driving the car, but there was no sign of dad, and mum was very tearful. She sat in the back with me and made a fuss of me all the way back to Christine and Dennis's house. As we travelled along, I was sure I'd see dad soon. When we arrived Dennis stopped the car, and we all got out, I looked to see dad coming out, but there was no sign of him.

Christine and the two dogs, Flash and Jess, were at the gate and they were very pleased to see me, but I avoided them. There was only one person I wanted to see and went through the door into the house sure that I would find him there. There was no sign of him anywhere; I went from room to room, but dad simply wasn't there. I lay down and watched and waited for him to come, but he never came.

I would hear conversations in which dads name was mentioned, but I couldn't understand what they were saying, I heard words like 'terrible' and 'awful' and 'surely somebody can do something', comments that I assumed were something to do with dad, but I just couldn't understand.

After a few weeks, I started to think, this must be like Whiskey, and that dad had died. As I convinced myself of this, I was filled with despair. My only thought was that if I too died then I will see him again, with this in mind, I laid down and stopped moving. I didn't eat my food or drink water, and I just waited for the end.

Mum tried to help me as did Dennis and Christine, but I was beyond help. Mum called the vet out in the hope that he would get me back on my feet. After examining me and just shook his head saying,

"I have only seen this very rarely, and I don't know why but this dog has simply lost the will to live."

Mum said, "After 16 years of being with him Lucky is waiting for my husband to come home, but he can't, for health reasons we don't know when he will be home and Lucky misses him".

Then the vet said, "Lucky is clearly dying from a broken heart."

"He may last a couple of days at most, but we can't bring him back from this".

mum said, "It is so cruel, I can't bear to see him suffer like this".

The vet replied, "The kindest thing to do would be to put him to sleep". Mum tearfully agreed. Then the vet said he is such big dog; perhaps I should muzzle him before I get the needle ready. Mum refused,

"You are not demeaning him like that, he is the gentlest dog who ever lived", she held me in her arms and told me that she loved me and that dad loved me, I never felt anything I just slipped away.

Final word from Dave Lodge (Dad)

This is the end of Lucky's story, but speaking as his friend and companion for 16 years I have to say that no more loyal dog ever lived. We did everything together throughout his life.

For my part, I have no hesitation in telling you that, from the moment he came into our lives, Lucky, Margaret and I enjoyed many happy days. They were joy filled days, precious memories that flood back as I share these recollections with you. We did always share Digestive Biscuits - they were our favourite.

We found Lucky dumped on the verge on the Mancunian Way the very busy elevated motorway that runs through the heart of Manchester. He had obviously been thrown from a moving car and was very fortunate to not have suffered major injuries. This event had a lasting effect for a long time afterwards - whenever the car we were travelling in came to a stop he'd have a tendency to be sick ... of course we were aware of this and were always well prepared with reassuring words and towels. He eventually overcame this fear with great patience, trust and understanding from both sides.

I had a different feeling about what happened on some occasions. So I will just tell you of some of his stories from my point of view.

When he ran into the foul smelling bog at Allonby Bay, I was reckless in the extreme when I ran in and picked him up. I had no idea how deep it was or if I could get out of it.

As Margaret said, I broke every rule I ever spoke about concerning rescuing dogs from the situations they sometimes get in to. My excuse was that Lucky was our friend, and so I reacted as I would if Margaret or a dear friend found themselves in similar trouble, I just plunged in. All I knew was I didn't want anything to happen that would cause me to be without my great companion.

Having said that, my advice is that you should not do what I did. Dogs have great survival instincts, and there are many cases of people jumping into rivers to save their dog and drowning, the dog then being found safe on the bank, later in the day.

Other incidents such as being stung by a nest of wasps, In that I can only praise Lucky for having the good sense to leave the area with great haste. More sense than me at the age of seven when a wasps nest fell on me from a crab apple tree. I was dancing on the spot, complaining to the man who came to my aid,

"Ee Lol, these flies have got hot feet"!

Lucky would not have been that silly he knew that the best thing to do was get home.

Indeed in my eyes he was a most remarkable dog who had no limit to his capabilities. He was very agile in his youth and did jump up and catch a bird in flight. He was so gentle as you have read, he could even carry an egg in his mouth without breaking it.

These traits enriched the lives of all the people who knew him. He is still spoken of in glowing terms many years after he passed away.

How many of us can truly claim to have achieved that kind of admiration in our life time? We continue to strive for the levels of loyalty, friendship and love that Lucky achieved. He will always be missed but never forgotten.

Following the accident that left me dependent on a walking stick, I was unable to leave the house. He was my constant companion and never complained about missing his three daily walks. Then when I could get out again, he matched my slow pace and never ran off or left me. Indeed, the reason I recovered to the level of fitness I did was because I didn't want to let Lucky down; so this encouraged me to walk as far as I could with him.

In the later account when I had to spend a prolonged time in the hospital, something had poisoned my system. The doctors never found out what it was. I was on various intravenous drips for nutrition, hydration and antibiotics as I could stomach neither food nor water. When I took Lucky for what did turn out to be his last walk with me and told him what a great dog he had been, I knew in my own heart that I was sinking fast and truly believed, that I would never recover from what ailed me.

There was no way Lucky would have been able to understand that, he would only know that his companion of many years was gone. So I do believe as the vet said that he gave up and died of a broken heart. I am very sad that I inadvertently became the cause of shortening his life.

He will continue to live in my heart till the day I die.

People who believe in reincarnation have suggested that Lucky has returned to us. I don't know enough about the subject of reincarnation to be sure that such things are possible; however, there are times when our latest family member Bruno cocks his head to one side and looks at me I feel I am seeing someone I have known before.

Lucky passed away at 1pm on the 20th August 2009. He was an intelligent and thoroughly lovely dog. His loss affected us deeply, and we missed him immensely. Filled with sadness, we started to reminisce about the adventures we shared and jotted them down. This book is the result.

I leave it up to you to decide the answer to the question Lucky asked at the start of his book:

"A dog can have a life story can't he"?

Lucky lived a great life in a wonderful way, and his story deserved to be told. I think that those of you who have shared their lives with a Lucky of your own will agree with me.

Family photo album

With Dad at Kirkoswald Church

Whiskey the cat

Bentley

Lucky with a chew stick

Lucky at 6 mont

Bruno & Harley

Lucky with Mum and Christine

Flash

Jess

Sheba

Lucky with Flash at Thornthwaite

Bassenthwaite Lake

The cottage at Bothel

With Sheba at Bassenthwaite Lake

Lucky with Flash at the Trout Hotel

Bruno in the car

Brandy

Dennis & Lucky

Oscar

International Praise for the author's previous books

Have Gravel Will Travel

Dave Lodge's biography about Tommy Bruce *Have Gravel Will Travel* is an excellent book. The reason it is an excellent book is because it doesn't just tell the very moving story about the life of sixties recording star Tommy Bruce. It also tells about what happened to some of the other sixties recording stars and where they are now. Artistes like Michael Cox, Lance Fortune and Nelson Keene, are in my minds eye again. I am reading *Have Gravel Will Travel* for the fourth time!!

Svein Sorlie Norway.

I believe Dave Lodge's book *Have Gravel will Travel* is more than just a fine tribute to our old mate Tommy Bruce. I think that in time it will come to be regarded as a reference point for the history of Rock and Roll history.

Brian Poole Hit Recording Artiste and Entertainer England

Dave Lodge with *Have Gravel will Travel* has written the best book about an entertainer Tommy Bruce, that I have ever read. The book made me see Tommy Bruce as a great guy who I would really like to have known. You just can not put this book down, page after page it just got more and more interesting.

John Eckert Talent Consultant, California, USA.

Have Gravel will Travel is a great book. Written by Dave Lodge I really enjoyed learning about sixties recording artiste Tommy Bruce. I just couldn't put this book down.

Manfred Kulman Author, Drummer, Rock and Roll Promoter. Beilfield, Scholenesh, Germany

Lucky A Dog's Tail

This book received special mention at the 2016 Lakeland Book of the Year awards! Lucky a Dogs Tail could move you to tears, I recommend that you read it.

Fiona Armstrong TV personality and book of the year judge.

Lucky A Dog's Tale is a read that will touch your heart, This time Dave Lodge shows the loyalty and friendship he and his dog Lucky shared for sixteen years. It is a clever piece of writing as Dave has written it from Lucky's perspective, as though Lucky had written it himself. **Great work. John Eckert. Talent Consultant. California. USA**

The Long Road

This a great read we get to know the people Dave Lodge has met as he journeys through life.

John Eckert Talent Consultant. USA

The Long Road also received special mention at The 2017 Lakeland Book of The Year. 'A very interesting read'

Hunter Davies. Event Judge and internationally respected author.

Crane The Left Handed Gun

Entered for the 2019 WWA Golden Spur Award.

Tin Pan Aspirations

Tin Pan Aspirations I always look forward to Dave Lodge's books and I have to say that *Tin Pan Aspirations* The Golly Goulding Story is one of Dave Lodge's best works to date. A very good read.

John Eckert. Talent Consultant, California USA.

Dave Lodge writes the kind of books that I enjoy reading. *The Long Road* and *Tin Pan Aspirations* open up the world of show business and the people in it. These two books follow on well from, *Have Gravel will Travel.* His book *Lucky A Dog's Tale* is different but still a good read.

Svein Sorlie Norway.

Chapel Of Dreams - The Peter Wynne Story

Peter Wynne was not only there at the beginning with the great names of British Rock and Roll in 1960, but he naturally possessed the kind of semi operatic vocal range that the likes of Elvis had to work on over two years in Germany! There is no doubt that Peter Wynne was one of the great voices of the sixties. He was the one to listen to, his effortless renditions of classic songs like

"More" and the beautiful ballad "For Your Love" Both of these songs were attempted in 1964 by Billy Fury, with whom Peter worked, will surely convince any sixties music lover of the excellence of this man's compelling voice.

Chris Ely-The sound of Fury

If like me you like to hear and read of people with great talent making their way in life with what seemed to be impossible dreams, then this book is the one for you. *Chapel of Dreams* gives you an insight to life of a man who knew he was born to make his way in life as a singer a man who will never give up, a man who will always be remember by that first Daily Express headline, 'The Voice of The Sixties'. I am sure that as you read and enjoy this very personal story, you will find that reading it, is worth every minute of your time.

Dave Lodge

Personal manager to the late Tommy Bruce.

DAVE AND MARGARET ARE LONG TIME SUPPORTERS OF THE DOGS TRUST AND GUIDE DOGS FOR THE BLIND.

WWW.DOGSTRUST.ORG.UK

WWW.GUIDEDOGS.ORG.UK

Dave Lodge's books range from novels to biographies and are available online and from good bookshops.

Have Gravel, will Travel

The Official Tommy Bruce Biography

The amazing story of how a young cockney lad went from 'barra boy' to a teen singing idol. A unique insight into the 1960's rock 'n' roll scene when Tommy Bruce and contemporaries such as Billy Fury, Johnny Kidd and Joe Brown were doing the rounds together. In this fickle world of show business many friendships don't stand the test of time. Not so that of Tommy Bruce and Dave Lodge, his manager, friend and author of this biography. We see how their partnership has endured since the 1960's unhampered by contracts, surviving on friendship through the highs and lows. The book is a testimony to Tommy's affable style both on and off stage making him a well-loved character in the industry for the past five decades.

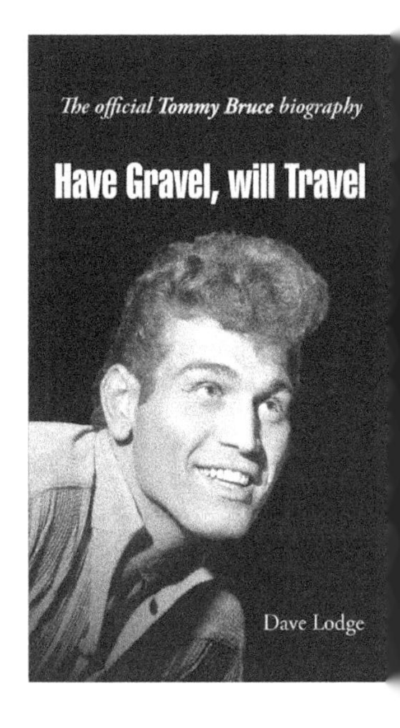

Price: £6.99

Paperback: 280 pages / 100 B&W photographs
Publisher: Pixel Tweaks Publications (July 2015)
ISBN-13: 978-0992751487

Lucky, a Dog's Tale

The story of a remarkable dog, whose loyalty and love for those in his life may have been equalled but never surpassed. From the moment he came into our lives, abandoned and dishevelled on the Mancunian Way, he was an amazing and unexpected addition to our family. A Newfoundland, Labrador cross, he grew to be a gentle giant who surprised us every day of his life.

This book will appeal to those who have enjoyed the company of wonderful pets of their own; they will understand how much we loved Lucky. I can't say he was the best dog in the world; I haven't known enough dogs to make that assumption, What I can say, without fear of contradiction is, "I have never known a better dog"!

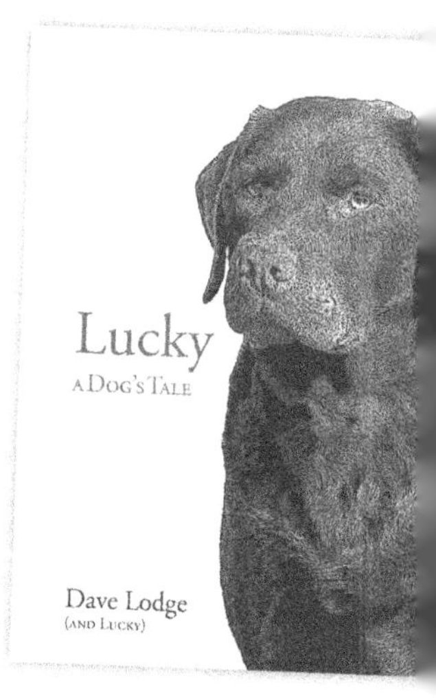

Lucky
A Dog's Tale
Dave Lodge
(and Lucky)

So I leave it up to you, read and enjoy Lucky's book and see if you can answer his question, "A dog can have a life story, can't he?"

Price: £4.99

Paperback: 72 pages with B&W photographs
ISBN-13: 978-09956190-3-6

CRANE

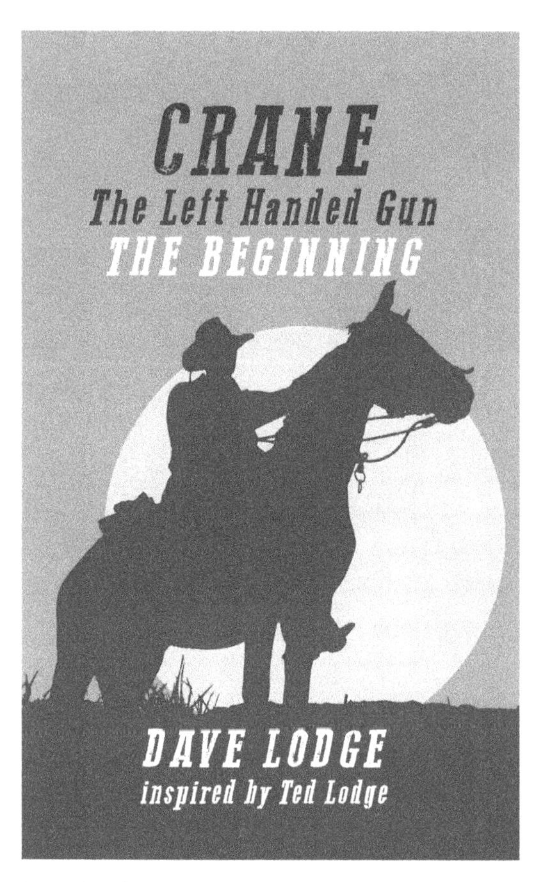

Born on a scrub farm o
Texas border, Crane is f
by circumstances to set
on the Vengence Trail.

He has his own code th
he would live and die b

Loyal and determined h
hope and love and frien
as he rides his lonely tra

With his horse Devil D
and his dog Bruno, he
havoc among the lawles
men who stalk the land

In this his fifth book D
Lodge manages to capt
the spirit of the Wild W
and has created a brand
hero in the form of To
Crane - the left handed

Paperback: 350 pages
Publisher: DML (9 April 2018)
Language: English
ISBN-13: 978-1999893682
Product Dimensions: 12.7 x 2 x 20.3 cm

CHAPEL OF DREAMS

pel of Dreams gives an insight
the life of a man who knew he
born to make his way as a singer.
an who will never give up, a man
will always be remembered by
first Daily Express headline,
: Voice of The Sixties".

ke me you like to read stories
ut people with great talent
ing their way in life with
ossible dreams, then this book is
ou. I am sure that as you read
enjoy this very personal story,
will find it worth every minute
ur time.

r Wynne was not only there at
eginning with the great names
ritish Rock and Roll in 1960,
he naturally possessed the semi
atic vocal range that Elvis had to
: on over two years in Germany!
e is no doubt that Peter Wynne
one of the great voices of the
es with effortless renditions
assic songs like More and the
tiful ballad For Your Love. Both
nich were attempted in 1964 by
Fury, with whom Peter worked.

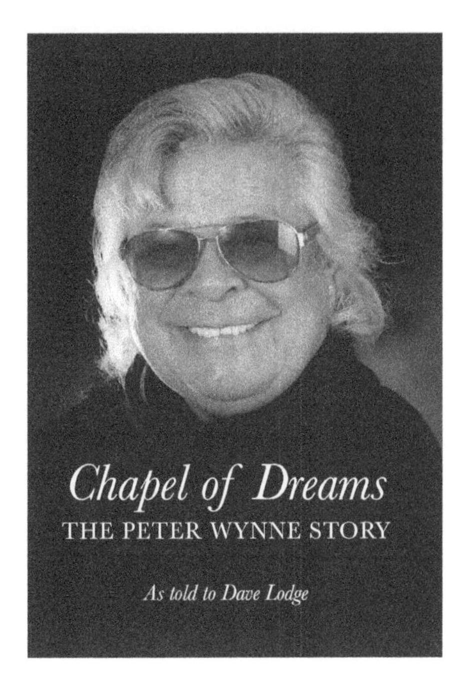

Chapel of Dreams
THE PETER WYNNE STORY
As told to Dave Lodge

Paperback: 412 pages
Publisher: DML (JAN 19)
Language: English
ISBN-13: 978-1916021709
Product Dimensions: 14.8 x 2.3 x 21 cm

Lightning Source UK Ltd.
Milton Keynes UK
UKHW020208131122
412093UK00003B/35